MISSIONARY KIDS

Who they are

Why they are who they are

What now?

Published in Australia
by Cypress Project

Cypress
Project

https://cypressproject.com.au

Dedication

To Juli, for the enduring bond of childhood friendship

and

to Lindsay, the soul-mate

who shares the colorful and divergent paths

of my adult sojourn.

Table of contents

Part 1: Who They Are

Part 2: Why They Are Who They Are

Part 3: What Now?

Vignettes & reflections from adult MKs

Chapter 1: **Missionary Kids (MKs) as Third Culture Kids (TCKs)**

Chapter 2: **Defining the third culture**

Chapter 3: **Outcomes of the MK childhood**

Chapter 4: **The MK's adult profile: identity and relationships**

Chapter 5: **The MK's adult profile: mobility and spirituality**

Chapter 6: **The developmental ecology shapes the MK**

Chapter 7: **More remote factors within the MK ecology**

Chapter 8: **Intervention into the MK ecology**

Chapter 9: **Relating to the adult MK**

Acknowledgements

I embarked on my doctoral program with the proactive plan of designing curriculum to nurture leadership enhancing qualities within those who had spent childhood years abroad. I saw leadership behaviors emerging naturally and I thought that educators in the international arena could make intentional efforts to nurture related qualities. However, the world of academics I had entered was not ready to accept that there even was a phenomenon related to children who grew up abroad so instead my research journey took me on the path of exploring adult outcomes that could be linked to childhood years spent abroad. The content of this book draws heavily upon the findings of that research. Dr. Irene Styles of Murdoch University contributed over and above the call of academic duty in the research and writing process of the initial work.

Personnel of Global Partners, the mission arm of The Wesleyan Church, contributed in significant ways to this work. Dr. Don Bray, Rev. Scott Olson, and Dr. John Connor read drafts of the manuscript and provided helpful feedback. Many missionary parents listened to my ideas and challenged my thoughts as I processed the content.

My parents, Walter and Dorothy Hotchkin, read and edited my vignettes, authenticating my recall and verifying time sequences.

A list of adult MKs, parents of MKs, and partners of MKs, whom I respect, took the time to write their own stories in support of various points within the text. Their names precede their stories. These stories are included with the permission of each author; they are a significant part of this text.

However, two people deserve the greatest acknowledgement: Juli Bray-Morris and Lindsay Cameron. Juli has been engaged at every step of the journey in compiling the content of this book. She not only read and commented on each chapter, she spent hours relating the concepts to her own experience and constructed many stories in support of the text. Lindsay read each draft, challenged each assertion, and then re-read each modification. Juli and Lindsay have been committed partners throughout this project and I acknowledge their significant contributions.

Introduction

I have never experienced any other childhood than that of the Missionary Kid (MK). I cannot, with integrity, describe the relative merits of being an MK or not being an MK. That is what I was born to in January 1966 while my parents were working as pioneer missionaries for the Wesleyan Church in Papua New Guinea (PNG). PNG was my birth place and my home until a month before I turned 18 years of age. A week after completing 12th grade, I flew to Australia with my parents in time to attend the wedding of my sister and in time to welcome the first child of my oldest brother and his wife.

I presented my passport at the Australian immigration counter, anticipating many changes in life as I took up residence in a foreign country that I had called my home country for the past 18 years. Nothing had prepared me for the enormity of the transition that lay ahead of me. PNG was and still is home to me; Australia is an excellent country for which to hold legal entitlement of residency.

There are not many significant choices to be made in the MK life. MKs follow their parents wherever their deployment and redeployments take them. My earliest memories are of the gently sloping contours of the Fugwa Wesleyan Mission station in the Southern Highlands of PNG. I was first brought there in a single engine plane flown by a Mission Aviation Fellowship pilot who transported my family back from the coastal town where I had been born. My two brothers and sister already called this place home. My father had built the timber structured house we lived in sometime after he and my mother, and two older brothers had first come to PNG in 1961. Single missionary teachers and nurses from Australia also lived at Fugwa to help with the development programs the Wesleyan Mission had established. Later, individuals and families came from the United States of America to join the work of the Wesleyan Mission in PNG.

Personal reflections on my early childhood are silhouetted against the morning sunshine and the afternoon rain showers of the Southern Highlands' weather patterns. My parents shared a strong friendship and they each took time to enjoy the four children God had brought to their home. The single missionaries were committed to their assignments and kept busy with the national people. However, when they came to our home my mother never failed to kindle a fire with dry sticks of wood in the big cast iron stove to boil water for a hot drink and conversation. These adults became our friends. They were both a witness and a contributor to the earliest days of my life. Some of them stayed on for as many years as I did in PNG and the friendship with these ones grew and matured.

My father arrived in PNG with a singleness of mind – to explain God's love and His gift of eternity through Jesus Christ to the people of PNG. PNG was a United Nations' mandated territory of Australia in 1961. The Australian government was given the task of coaching the country of PNG toward self-government within the international political arena. The task was huge for a country that itself boasted a population of less than 20 million people. Mission agencies were invited to contribute to the development of PNG and so each interested denominational group petitioned for an area within which to engage to bring medical and educational development. The missionary teachers and nurses managed this work and my father preached. At first, he had no language to share his love of God, so he prayed. As he learned the language and as he developed friendships with those who could translate, his preaching ministry increased. He would walk from village to village preaching. He would bring in those whom he was discipling to teach them a new biblical lesson each week that they could then share with others back in their own villages.

My parents' first love was God. Their children were a close second. We knew we were cherished. Both my brothers learned to craft wooden things with their hands because my father knew how to work with timber. Both the boys grew up learning from my father. All three were meticulously careful in the finished product of their timber work. My father shared his knowledge of the Bible in words we could understand and all four of us grew up with a love of God. We learned to pray but were never forced into meaningless ritual. Both my parents talked of a God that could be understood and modeled a life that reflected a meaningful and relevant relationship with God. We were encouraged to express our questions about Christianity and no issue had to be immediately resolved if there seemed to be no meaningful answer. A love of God grew out of personal conviction.

The march of time brings with it challenges and painful choices for any family. Separation was one of the greatest challenges for our family. My childhood memories of my oldest brother are compartmentalized to the school holidays surrounding Christmas. A few weeks after my birth my brother flew back to the boarding home where he lived to attend an international school. He came home each school holidays until he entered high school. He had to go to Australia to attend high school and only came home during the Christmas break. My second brother attended school a little closer to home but still boarded away from home during the week and later during the term. My sister and I were companions throughout childhood even when we both went to a boarding home ourselves at the ages of ten and eight respectively. Two years later my sister had to move to a different town in order to further her schooling. That year we were boarding in three different places, my oldest brother in Australia, my second brother and my sister in one town, and me in another. The Christmas school holidays were a celebration in the life of our family because we were all back together for the few short weeks.

By the time I was 14 years of age each of my siblings had taken up residence in Australia. During the remaining four years of my MK childhood I learned a lot about friendship and about extreme Christian living. I was living with my parents by this stage. Their ministry had brought them to the urban area where I had been attending elementary school. A high school had, by now, been established to service the children of missionaries. My father had retained his singleness of mind and was still preaching and teaching the people of PNG about God's love and eternity with Him through a commitment to Christ. He traveled, discipled, preached, and encouraged the growing number of national pastors within our denomination in their various places of ministry. My mother had her own discipleship ministry and she managed the finances for the mission.

My MK life, for the last four years in PNG, revolved around school and the youth group run by some of the younger missionaries. I'd accepted the Christian faith as my own at the age of nine. When I was 13, I took some classes offered by one of the Wesleyan missionaries to confirm my understanding of the fundamentals of Christian teaching; at the end of the classes I was baptized. A week later I came into junior membership in the Wesleyan Church, along with four other MKs. Those early decisions have been reference-points in my life, against which subsequent choices and options have been weighed.

I was privileged to attend high school where the MKs were the majority. We were raised to be strongly evangelical and those who came into our midst, who did not already have a significant understanding of the Christian faith, soon had the basics shared with them. I absorbed the teaching and discipleship of the young missionaries who were our teachers and those who ran the youth group for us. I tried to emulate the daily disciplines of the Christian faith I saw and heard about from them. These young missionaries took the time to arrange activities that provided safe boundaries within which the other MKs and I could explore our emerging and alternative identities. These young adults had given up the pursuit of professional and financial ambition in order to serve God and the people of PNG. I was privileged to come under their intentional and unintentional discipleship.

I am a product of my childhood. I inherited many traits from my parents. I am both alike and unalike each of my three siblings. There are many inherited traits that we share and there are many values and characteristics we share as a result of our unusual childhood. We have, however, each responded to our childhood in different ways. One thing we share is that we each emerged from childhood with a mature Christian faith. My second brother passed into God's presence when he was 36 years of age, having fought bone cancer for four years. During his final year of life, he shared with me on a number of occasions, descriptions of heaven as he saw it in visions God gave to him. He knew he was ready to be in God's presence. The three of us still living have continued to serve God and the Wesleyan Church in different ways. Each of us has been in pastoral ministry with our respective spouses; two of us have served as missionaries with the Wesleyan Church; two of us have worked within humanitarian and development needs on behalf of the Church. We each have a lifelong commitment to God and to the Wesleyan Church.

I am a product of my childhood and I reflect positively upon the MK experience. I have taken root and grown in the garden in which God planted me, the Wesleyan Church. I am able to reflect honestly about the challenges and pain of my childhood experiences. I am also able to make meaning and sense out of my experiences both in terms of social and spiritual development. There are those who try to explain to me that my parents made wrong choices about the childhood they gave to me and my siblings. There are those who feel God can achieve the Great Commission without considerable cost to individuals and families. I have to accept our differing paradigms of understanding.

I am aware that there are many others who reflect with great pain upon their own MK years or the years during which they were raising MKs. Sometimes the MK experiences have involved extreme environments or choices with which adults or children have had to deal. I, in no way, negate the experiences of these individuals. I listen with empathy whenever an individual chooses to share with me, their pained reflections. With some of them I cry, with some I feel free to challenge them to look beyond the pain. With all of them I want to ask about a relationship with God borne from personal conviction.

This book is presented with my own grounded and constructive perspective of the MK life as a backdrop to every thought and reflection. My prayer is that it will be a productive contribution to the mission arena. I pray that it will not add further pain to those who suffer with their MK, or parent-of-MK reflections. May heaven rejoice in the many that are brought to a genuine knowledge and conviction of the Christian faith by the work that is accomplished through missionary families, and within the homes of missionary families.

<h1 style="text-align:center;"><u>Part 1: Who they are</u></h1>

Chapter 1: **Missionary Kids (MKs) as Third Culture Kids (TCKs)**

An Average Childhood

How does one define an average childhood? Does it equate to: a loving family, a solid education, constructive discipline, toys, pets, sports, art and cultural development, celebrating life's milestones with extended family?

Perhaps an average childhood is simply what those around you, who are most involved in your developmental years, also experience. It is believed to be average because it is familiar or shared. The children of missionary personnel might define their childhood as average. Those around them are experiencing the same life patterns as they themselves are and so the experience seems average. They may not be aware of the exceptions their childhood experiences pose when compared to the average childhood experienced in their passport country.

An average childhood for a Missionary Kid (MK) equates to: a loving family (sometimes separated by miles or continents); a solid education (often taking place in multiple school settings in different countries and different continents); constructive discipline (sometimes administered by a variety of caregivers whose boundaries and tolerances vary); toys (bearing relevance to multiple cultures); pets (many times left behind or left in the care of others for extended periods when the MK relocates); sports (often involving disrupted coaching and development); art and culture (sometimes involving exposure to a vast array of what is pleasing and what is acceptable in a given society); celebrating life's milestones with extended family (usually inclusive of a surrogate extended family drawn from the broader mission personnel working in the same location).

MKs are not the only children who are impacted by such exceptional but shared developmental experiences. The children of foreign deployed government diplomats, military personnel, humanitarian workers, and private business people are also affected by the time spent abroad. The children drawn from each of these categories all experience childhood environments and life patterns distinct from those of age equivalent peers in their passport countries. They learn behaviors in response to these life patterns. The learned behaviors become so embedded in the overall make-up of these individuals that they impact the adult profile. These learned behaviors unite these individuals into a group recognized as Third Culture Kids or TCKs. They are set apart from the individuals who have been raised within one culture because they have learned to negotiate at least two cultures, the culture of their passport country and that of their host country. They are set apart from immigrants and refugees because they have grown up knowing that they would eventually repatriate to the passport country of a parent or parents. Their childhood is unique but shared. A TCK, no matter where he or she has grown up, or what mix of cultures has impacted his or her childhood can relate to another TCK. They have a shared culture and have a natural affinity with one another.

How is it possible that a Canadian who spent childhood years in Kenya can have a shared culture with a New Zealander who spent childhood years in the Solomon Islands, and a Korean who spent childhood years in South Africa? How can these individuals have an affinity both as children and as adults? Furthermore, how is it that they can share common profile traits in their adult years? These questions need answers, for those who experience the TCK life, for those who walk through it with them, and later in life for those who seek to understand the adult choices made and values held by these individuals.

Growing up abroad... Rosalea as a teacher in Africa

George walked into the room with a bag slung over his back, an infectious grin on his face, and a soccer ball under his arm. George had just arrived from Tanzania and was joining the fifth-grade class I was teaching part way through the school year. I surveyed the room to determine where to place him amidst the students already seated at the desks that I had carefully positioned around the room to facilitate cooperative learning. Was he going to be an English as a Second Language learner? I didn't think so because Tanzania used English as their medium of education. I wondered what his learning strengths and weaknesses were so that I could team him with a group who could help him settle in, relate to his passions, and support him in areas of challenge. I briefly surveyed the casual stance, the friendly smile, and the muscle toned physique. The soccer ball was the decider. I invited him to take a seat at the table with Simon*, Kirsty*, Abu*, and Mabiza*.*

Simon was from Costa Rica and he lived for break times and the chance to challenge anyone at soccer. Simon struggled in most areas of learning. So far, his schooling had been in Spanish and his mother didn't speak any English. His adoptive father came home from work late and had to divide his time between the two school aged children and their needs with homework assistance. Simon was a happy child until backed into a vulnerable position where he became acutely aware of his learning disadvantage and then he was unreasonable. I was making progress with him academically and helping him to manage his behavior better as he grew in self-awareness. Simon and George would connect via the soccer ball!

Kirsty was a self-confident Dutch girl. She was very popular amongst the teachers because she was a high achiever both in academics and sports, articulate in public speaking roles, attractive and socially competent. Kirsty attended Dutch School several afternoons each week so that she could maintain an academic standard in that language to ensure her success when her family moved back to Holland. Kirsty did not struggle with this academic pressure as did some of the other Dutch children in the community. Kirsty could, however, be a little condescending toward others less competent than herself. I'd placed her with Simon because Simon exceeded her sporting competencies but needed her academic support in the classroom. I'd placed her with Mabiza so she could learn from his quiet manner while being challenged by his capabilities. Kirsty was growing in tolerance, kindness, and in her ability to help others develop.

Abu was the friendliest child in the class. He liked everyone and saw good in whomever he met. Abu had been born in Mozambique, the country where my classroom was situated, part of the Maputo International School. Abu's father was Portuguese and his mother was Norwegian. He was fluent in both languages. His best friend from Preschool days was from Argentina. Abu's parents worked long hours and traveled frequently so he spent a lot of time in the home of his friend. Abu was fluent in Spanish. He had a 3-year-old sister whom he adored and would parade around the school corridors whenever his mother brought her to the school. The young sister had devised her own lingo from the conglomeration of sounds she heard in communication in the home, so Abu related to her using the sounds that she found meaningful. Abu found academics a challenge. He seldom had the full complement of equipment needed for school activities and he regularly misplaced books and notes. Home was not an organized place. However, Abu brought a heightened value of tolerance and a passion for inclusiveness to our classroom. Simon, Kirsty, and Mabiza were all maturing because of his presence at their table.

And then there was Mabiza, a small, quietly spoken child with a sharp, analytical mind. He spoke up seldom but always contributed in depth when called upon in class. He did well in every area of schooling, obviously coming from a home where there was an abundance of educational stimulation without unreasonable pressure to perform. Mabiza was also very nimble and kept pace with the other soccer obsessed students in the school. Mabiza was from Tanzania and I hoped George would feel comfortable with someone else from his home country.

I now had 16 children in my class representing 15 different nationalities. George and Mabiza, each from Tanzania, was the first duplication of nationalities. Our learning environment was rich. I valued each day as a teacher. Each day was a new opportunity to help my students excel as learners, as responsible and caring individuals, and as observant global citizens. From their many different countries, and from their vastly diverse socio-economic home lives, they were learning to value each other. They understood each other's challenges. Together they were shaping one another's value systems, worldviews, and emerging identities. (*Names have been changed.)

These were Third Culture Kids.

These unusual environments are replicated around the world in internationals schools and in settings where foreign people are deployed and form collectives. No matter the location around the globe, the children in these settings recognize each other's behavior patterns in response to their unusual lives. The TCKs from this context could relate as easily to individuals who have experienced the same environment in another geographic location. Later, as adults they are comfortable with each other, finding an immediate connection, understanding why they share a high value of tolerance, a broad world view, a need to help others, a passion for inclusiveness. Location has not shaped these shared values but rather the patterns of life have formed the boundaries of the Third Culture and facilitated the affinity between these individuals both as children and as adults.

A growing body of research addresses the TCK phenomenon and yet there is still very little written about it in general literature. This book provides some descriptions about what research has found about the Third Culture and about the adult profile of individuals who experience the Third Culture. The focus is on the experience of missionary children.

The book progresses through three stages in describing the outcomes and the factors of significance in the MK life: Who they are; Why they are who they are; What now?

Who they are...

We look at what research suggests are some of the shared adult traits of MKs. What are the characteristics they recognize in each other as children and as adults? What are the similar values and life trajectory choices they make that define them and establish the unspoken understanding between members of this sub-culture?

Why they are who they are...

We look at the factors of significance that create the unique MK developmental context. These are the factors that are common to all, or most Third Culture MK contexts and define it as a shared childhood environment. These are the factors that leave an indelible imprint in the developing individual and ultimately result in the adult profile.

What now?

We propose some constructive intervention to maximize the MK childhood experience. We respond to the concerns of those who want to provide the best nurturing environment for the children of missionary personnel. We respond to the concerns of parents, spouses, close friends, and missionary associates who interact with adult MKs.

The purpose of this book is to provide a framework for understanding the MK experience both as it unfolds and as it impacts the remainder of life. Although based upon research findings it also draws upon real life experiences and upon what is available in published literature. The book is intended to be a readable book for the general population interested in the MK experience, rather than an academic work. A full description of the academic works upon which findings have been drawn is included in the Notes at the end of the book[1].

Chapter 2: **Defining the Third Culture**

Third Culture Kids (TCKs)

Children who grow up outside their parents' home country, but expect to repatriate to it, have been defined as Third Culture Kids or TCKs.[1] TCKs spend a significant period of their childhood abroad. The time spent abroad may be one year or eighteen, and the long-term impact of the experience may be proportionate to the length and intensity of the experience. However, they are all TCKs.

It is important to distinguish TCKs as a specific category because the uniqueness of their developmental experience has a long-term impact and the adult outcomes can be traced back to the specific context of their childhood. The experience of TCKs has some resemblance to that of biracial children who are affected, throughout childhood, by two parental cultures. However, it is distinguishable because the TCK has an inherent connection with the passport country but does not have an inherent connection with the host country. For the biracial child the passport country and the host country are usually one and the same.

The TCK experience has some resemblance to the experience of refugees and immigrants because there is a need to learn the ways of a new host culture. However, it is distinguishable because the TCK lives with the expectation of repatriation to the parents' home country. In the case of biracial parentage, where the child is being raised in a country foreign to either parent, the TCK lives with the expectation of repatriation to one or another parental home country. There is seldom the expectation that the child will remain in the host country. Immigrant and refugee children do not live with the certainty of repatriation. Therefore, a Third Culture Kid is one who spends childhood years outside the parents' home country but expects to repatriate to it. A Missionary Kid or MK is a TCK who spends childhood years outside the parents' home country for the purpose of missionary work, but lives with the expectation of repatriation to a parental home country.

> A Third Culture Kid is one who spends
> childhood years outside the parents' home
> country, but expects to repatriate to it.

Other TCKs may belong to sub-categories that reflect families deployed abroad for the purpose of government diplomatic engagement, military service, humanitarian work, or private business ventures. Each sub-category has its defining factors. This work focuses on the unique elements affecting the MK childhood.

I am a TCK...*Juli reflecting as an adult*

The first ten years of my life were spent in Papua New Guinea. I left Grand Rapids, Michigan at 18 months and returned to the U.S.A the summer before I entered fifth grade. My family traveled back to the States taking a month to visit Australia, Southeast Asia, England and Europe. During my first few weeks back, a church friend prayed with me that I would lose my Australian accent so that I would not be made fun of by my peers. I recall feeling shocked that my accent would ever be considered a social flaw. I had just moved from a school where the students in my class were Australians, Japanese, British, Tongans, Europeans and a few Americans. I had no file in which to register this new information that people in the Midwest did not like accents. I recall telling a fifth-grade teacher who was angry that I did not know Indiana history that, in fact until a few months previous, I had not even known there was an Indiana. What I did not mention was that for much of my young life, I thought America was in Europe.

Once in the States, I worked hard to assimilate but never did so successfully. By the time I was a senior in high school, my companions became the exchange students who were currently living as TCKs. I hung out with young women from Germany, the Netherlands, and Columbia and young men from Belgium and Brazil. In discovering this group of students, I felt as if I had "come home" to a part of myself. The Third Culture identity stepped forward intrinsically. In college, I found that most of the people I gravitated toward had some sort of Third Culture identity. Even now as in my thirties, most of my closest friends spent a portion of their lives outside their passport culture.

The Third Culture

If these children are Third Culture Kids, one necessarily asks: What is the Third Culture? The Third Culture cannot be simply defined, rather, it needs to be unwrapped. One must reach an accepted concept of culture before one can absorb an understanding of the Third Culture.

Culture is a shared way of living.[2] Culture is a body of learned behaviors common to a given human society or collection of people. People learn culture, it is not inherent in an individual. Many qualities are transmitted genetically like hair color, bone structure, and a baby's desire for food in the morning. These are physiological characteristics found in the human genetic code.

> Culture is a body of learned behaviors
> common to a given human society or
> collection of people. People learn culture, it
> is not inherent in an individual.

The typical breakfast food chosen by adults in a given society however, cannot be connected to genetic make-up. It is instead, a learned (cultural) response to the desire for food in the morning. In one culture adults may choose to eat bread and drink hot tea while in another culture morning hunger may be abated by eating cold sweet potato cooked the night before and accompanied by a drink of cold water. In yet another culture, adults may breakfast on processed cereal, buttered toast, and hot coffee. In each instance the chosen behavior seems automatic and natural but it has, in fact, been learned over time. From earliest years, specific breakfast foods have been offered to the child who has gradually grown accustomed to that way of satisfying morning hunger. It seems natural. Experiencing an alternative seems unnatural.

Another example might be patterns of speech that are learned and adopted over time. Most babies are born with the capacity to make sound but the sounds that are learned are those that are heard and imitated from the surrounding environment. Making sound comes naturally as part of the human genetic code. The auditory shapes those sounds take are learned (cultural) behavior. This not only applies to the language or languages a child adopts but also the accent and the context specific colloquialisms that become part of conversational speech. By the time the child reaches adulthood it is almost impossible to entirely reshape these deeply embedded learned behaviors. Such learned behaviors represent the individual's culture. They are not characteristics inherent from birth but they are equally defining of the person as an individual and as a member of a human collective.

Culture is shaped by environment. The Third Culture is shaped by environment. That environment includes many defining elements, amongst them is awareness that the world is complex and embraces many different people groups from many different places.

Awareness of a complex world...Juli reflecting as an adult

When I returned to live in the States, at the age of ten, I had to learn to navigate a new culture. I recall my fifth-grade teacher placing me in the rudimentary reading group because of my poor spelling (and my lack of Indiana history, I presume). This was outrageous to me because I had always been in the accelerated groups. I responded as some children do who are under-challenged and became a behavior problem. I had moved from a multi-cultural environment to an almost exclusively mono-cultural one and I felt lost and misunderstood. That year I met a boy in our school from Laos. On the swing set, in broken English, he told me his story of loss and trauma, and while we did not look alike or sound alike, I could connect with him in a way I could not with other children. Not because of loss or hardship, but because of shared awareness that the world is made up of many different people and many different places.

Children acquire behavior patterns in response to what they have experienced whether it is loss and hardship, or removal from one location that has been home to another location that is presumed to be home in an alternative paradigm of understanding.

Early definitions of the Third Culture described the impact of two cultures on the developing child, the shared way of living from the parents' home country, and the shared way of living from the host country (Figure 2.1).[3] The early suggestions were that the children of foreign deployed personnel existed in a culture created by an intersecting of the two cultures. TCKs were presumed to adopt some qualities from each culture and thereby create their own, Third Culture.

Figure 2.1 Early representation of the Third Culture[4]

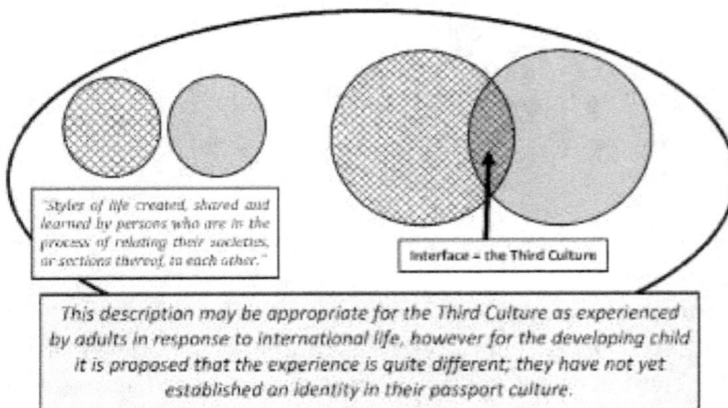

However, this definition did not account for the affinity shared between all TCKs no matter what their passport or parents' home country, or their host country. Nor did it adequately explain the experience of those children who had been born abroad and had not, themselves significantly experienced the parents' home culture. The intersecting of two cultures can at best describe the experience of the adults deployed abroad who choose to adopt some of the host country culture.

So, if it is not an intersecting of a passport and a host culture, what is the Third Culture?

The Third Culture is the collection of behavior that reflects a response to the environment experienced by children who grow up abroad but expect to repatriate to a parent's home country. It is the collection of learned behavior in response to the patterns of life experienced by all TCKs no matter where they are born, where their parents come from, or where they spend their childhood years. The Third Culture is the collection of learned behavior that seems natural according to life as they have experienced it. Just as the processed breakfast cereal and hot coffee in the morning seem natural to some adults, so the responses to life that result from childhood experiences come naturally to the TCK. There are shared patterns of life that children who grow up abroad experience no matter what host country they live in or what passport country they claim. The learned behaviors that come naturally in response to the shared life patterns represent the culture.

> The learned behaviors that come naturally
> in response to the shared life patterns
> represent the culture.

To comprehend the collection of learned behavior resulting from the TCK experience, it is essential first to establish the factors of significance that define the childhood environment, setting it apart from the experience of the child raised within the cultural context of his or her own parents. What are those defining elements?

It is useful at this point to begin to use the term ecology rather than environment to describe the factors of significance surrounding the TCK. The term environment refers to external elements that surround a person, animal, or plant. Ecology on the other hand refers to the relationships between living things and the surrounding elements. The significance of interaction is included in the term ecology. This is an important distinction because the developing child, the TCK, engages and interacts with the defining elements of the childhood experience. The external elements in the child's life are not static and the child is not passive toward those elements. There is a force between the child and the elements. It is in these dynamic processes that character is shaped.

Ecology can be represented by a series of concentric circles (Figure 2.2) with the child, the emerging individual, at the center. The child contributes to the ecology and interacts with other elements of the ecology. The context is dynamic. There are causes and effects. There are happenings and responses to those happenings. Ecology is not static. The elements within it interact and produce outcomes.

Figure 2.2 An adapted model, proposed to depict the Third Culture Kid (TCK) ecology of human development[5]

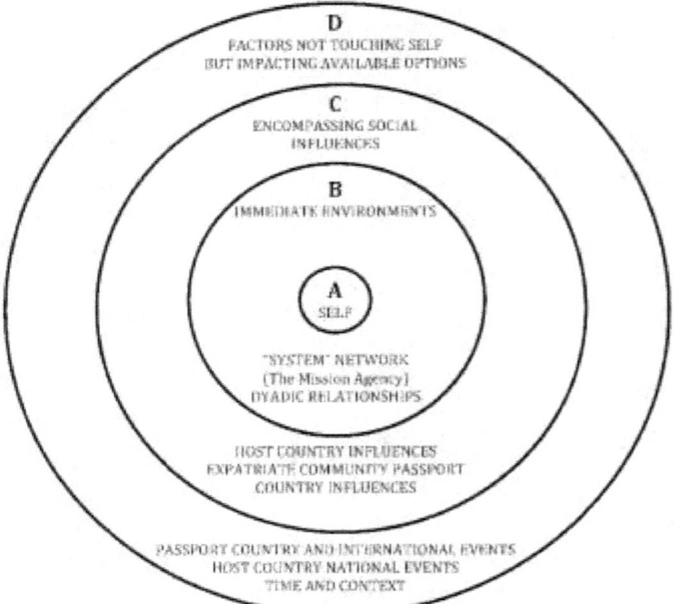

Ecology begins with the child as Self: likes, dislikes, social and anti-social disposition, strengths and weaknesses. Ecology expands to encompass the immediate surroundings physically and socially: the home, family members, interaction styles and relational patterns within those immediate surrounds. Even within a single family there is a variety of likes and dislikes, social and anti-social behavior styles. A given location will impact one child differently to another. A given adult personality within the ecology will relate better to one child than to another. Ecology is dynamic and each child experiences and responds to the surrounding elements.

Ecology expands further to encompass ever widening layers of physical surroundings and gradually more complex interactions and relational patterns that demand more from Self. The child engages in social and cultural development, sport and recreation that involve mixing with a growing number of adults and children. The child's friendship network broadens and there are more and more non-familial adults who become significant to the child. For the MK these are often drawn from the mission agency with whom his or her parents are employed as well as personnel of other mission agencies working in the same location.

At the extremity of ecology there is the impact of historical context. Each life is lived within an historical era and significant things happen that indirectly shape a child's development. This includes progressive achievements in technology such as multimedia advances that change the way communication is relayed around the world. It includes political stability in the passport and host countries. The onset or culmination of war within countries is of significance. It includes gender opportunities and religious tolerances.

Self does not interact with the factors represented at the extremity of the ecology but the impact of them on development is significant. For example, access to electronic mail has a significant impact on the interaction style of MKs with their family and friends. The development of MKs in this decade is vastly different to that of MKs from two or three decades ago when there could be many weeks between a response to a question asked in a posted letter. Another example is the role the United States is playing in the world arena and the impact this has on the perception of globally deployed USA personnel. Pro or anti USA sentiments shape USA MK development and those MKs who represent USA allied nations.

Understanding ecology is important in comprehending the uniqueness and defining elements of the TCK experience and the eventual outcome that shapes the adult profile of individuals who experience it. The factors of significance for the MK include physical factors but also relational opportunities that are distinct. Individuals engage and choose patterns of response to the ecology as a whole. These include responses to the physical experience but also to the presenting relational opportunities. Consistently and over time these defining elements shape the MK. The adult profile is impacted and character traits are embedded

Figure 2.2 provides a general outline of the ever-broadening dimensions of the MK ecology of development. Individuals can themselves apply the model to their own particular context in order to identify personalized elements and people of significance.

Having detailed the elements and people of significance, an individual can then begin to examine the responses to these factors within the ecology of development.

My ecology of development...Juli reflecting as an adult

A	Self	Me, age 9, gregarious, moody, active, artistic
B	Immediate environments	Boarding hostel in Mt. Hagen, with biological parents as house parents, ten to thirteen kids in the hostel, the domestic worker, Hongoi, government day school for internationals, English and Pidgin church
C	Encompassing but more remote influences	Drinking and tribal unrest, PNG Independence, dressing up for Halloween and visiting a few expatriate homes for candy
D	Factors not touching self but impacting available options.	Watergate and Vietnam, Space programs, Cold War

Learned Behavior in Response to Life Patterns

From childhood, individuals learn to negotiate the patterns of life they experience and the relationships within those life patterns. They develop skills and capacities that help them adapt to the demands of life. In a remote African village, a young girl learns to juggle an infant sibling strapped to her back while she collects water and fire wood to help her mother prepare the evening meal. In the urban bustle of an Australian city a young boy learns to catch public transport to attend a reputable school. Neither could respond competently to the demands of the other child's life. Over time each child has acquired learned behavior to manage what society demands within the specific context. Likewise, the TCK acquires a collection of learned behaviors in response to the parameters of his or her childhood ecology. In the case of TCKs, location has not defined these parameters, rather it is the shared patterns of life that define the parameters.

> It is the shared patterns of life that
> define the parameters.

It does not matter where the TCK childhood is spent, whether it is in France, Ethiopia, Japan, or the USA, it is the patterns of life that define the developmental ecology. It is in the context of negotiating at least two countries, holding a passport for one country while spending childhood years in another, absorbing the nurture of caregivers drawn from a number of different cultures, and processing an autonomous identity while holding an allegiance to more than one nation. These complexities define the parameters of the TCK ecology and impact the adult profile of Third Culture Kids.

The TCK learns that it is a courtesy and in fact pragmatic to scan the room to determine the highest representation before deciding which language he or she should use to address a particular social group. The TCK learns that it is best not to accumulate material goods because you can be sure that you will have to sort, pack and move again before too long. The TCK learns to attach sentiment to a select few objects that become symbolic of the places one has lived. The TCK learns to negotiate international travel and learns patterns of leave taking from friends from an early age. The child raised within the cultural context of his or her own parents could not respond competently to the demands of the TCK life. Over time the TCK has acquired learned behavior to manage the demands of this pattern of life.

The learned responses may vary somewhat but they are still recognizable to another TCK and there is sufficient commonality that the individuals can be recognized as part of a cultural group. This is the Third Culture. A TCK has an immediate affinity with another TCK because of the shared patterns of life and the collection of learned behavior in response to those life patterns. Although they may not have shared a childhood location, they have experienced the same childhood ecology and the impact of those defining elements has left an indelible imprint on the adult profile of the TCK. For TCKs there is an ability to communicate with each other about childhood experiences and subsequent life choices in a manner that excludes those who have not shared the Third Culture. This is the affinity that TCKs share. Sub-categories of TCKs such as MKs, experience even more closely aligned life patterns and the affinity can be stronger.

In the next chapter we explore the adult profile of the Missionary Kid as it emerges from the TCK ecology. In subsequent chapters we will return to the discussion of this unique developmental ecology and explore more specifically how it shapes the lives of those individuals who experience childhood years within it.

Chapter 3: **Outcomes of the MK childhood**

The MK Developmental Ecology

Missionary Kids know why they are growing up outside their parents' home country. From earliest years their parents and their parents' co-workers explain to them that God has given their families special tasks to do that involve living in a foreign country. God is part of the MK's psyche from as early as the MK can recall. If the MK is old enough to discuss the transition before the family moves abroad then there is interaction about what to expect, where the family will be living, how he or she will be schooled and the many other changes that lie ahead. If the MK is an infant, or born abroad, then the God-factor of missionary life is part of his or her emerging vocabulary. It forms a backdrop in the formation of his or her worldview. God and His Great Commission is the reason for MK life.

> God and His Great Commission
> is the reason for MK life.

God and His Great Commission influence who the MK becomes as an emerging individual. The God-factor is the singularly defining element of the MK childhood ecology that sets the MK apart from other TCKs.

Although MKs know why they are growing up abroad they cannot necessarily articulate what is other than average about their childhood. As suggested in the Chapter 1, perhaps average is just what those around you who are most involved in your developmental years also experience. Other MKs are also impacted by the issues that define the Third Culture and the added God-factor.

The MK develops a vocabulary and behaviors that facilitate competent negotiation of these defining factors of life but the MK cannot necessarily articulate these as factors of significance that shape his or her world. The young African girl with the sibling strapped to her back while carrying out household chores has the relevant vocabulary and competence to function within her role but she could probably not articulate the unique expectations upon her. Children grow up unaware of what shapes their worldview and the collective learned behaviors that define their culture. Later in life MKs reflect on their childhood and they are better able to articulate the defining elements of their childhood ecology and the significant impact that ecology had in shaping their adult profile.

There may be isolated moments during childhood when an MK becomes aware that life has some unusual elements for him or her to negotiate or reconcile but young children at least seldom dwell long upon these realizations.

*Where I am from...*Rosalea as a child

Sitting on the beach, scratching in the soft white sand, watching the waves roll in from the Pacific Ocean, I think about the morning visit to the hospital where I was born. I am baby number S341 who was registered with the Australian government in the Territory of New Guinea, delivered in the Wewak hospital by a nurse because the doctor was at lunch.

Wewak is a beautiful coastal town, a town I have not been to since my birth. My two older brothers and my sister are also from Wewak because they have each been to boarding school in this town. My sister was born in Madang, another beautiful coastal town edging up to the Pacific Ocean. We had a family holiday there one other year so I saw where she was born two years before me. At the time of her birth that was the hospital with the best reputation. When I was born, Wewak was the choice. One of my friends is from Goroka because the hospital there had been the best in another year.

But my two brothers are from Australia because that was where they were born. I wasn't sure about that, though. I tried to think it through as I watched my family members body-surfing the waves and swimming further out. The waves frightened me. I'd been surprised by the power of the water pushing down on me as I got caught in a turning wave. Each of my siblings had lived in Wewak and they all had friends here. I lived in Mt. Hagen, a town in the highlands of Papua New Guinea, and all my friends were there. The night before we'd had an evening meal with a family whose children were school friends with my sister and brother. Today as we drove around the town my oldest brother had pointed out places where he had spent time and where he had gone to school, when he lived here some years ago.

Were my brothers from Wewak or Australia? I knew my oldest brother was from Australia because he lived there to go to university. I knew my second brother would move there soon because he was close to the end of school.

I remember visiting Australia once and meeting my parents' relatives. There were a lot of them. My Dad's brothers and sisters organized a picnic in a park and there were more than 30 cousins. I didn't know any of them so stuck with my sister for the afternoon. We did play a game of cricket and everyone was very friendly. But I missed Juli, Juline, Karen, Mary, Christina, Martha, Ruth, Auntie Fran, and Auntie Delwynne. I wondered what they were doing back in Papua New Guinea and couldn't wait to get back home where I knew everyone and knew how to act; where I belonged. I wondered if all my friends back there also had relatives in another country and if they knew how it felt not to belong sometimes.

My parents had been talking about getting the paperwork to have my sister and I naturalized so that we would each have a document saying we were Australian even though we had been born in a different country. It didn't mean anything to me but I figured it must be important because they said it had to be done before Papua New Guinea was granted independence as a nation and set up self-government. From what I could tell it wasn't going to change anything for me, so I put all those thoughts out of my mind.

I loved my life. I did miss my brothers and sister when they weren't around, which was most of the year because we all lived away from home to go to school. But the holidays were fun. My brothers were happy, energetic people and made time to do things with me when we were back home on the mission compound with my parents. There, my sister and I shared a room and caught up on the time lost. Maybe the mission compound was where home really was? Or was it at the boarding hostel where I had responsibilities and a protective relationship with my younger co-boarders.

Eventually I gave up thinking about all these things and decided to try the waves again. It really didn't matter; I'd figure it out later if and when it needed a simple answer. For now, I wanted to see if one of my brothers would teach me to swim.

Most young children accept and enjoy the immediate context within which they are immersed. They are naïve to the fact that the day to day routines of life, the interactions both simple and complex, the choices that are made for and by them are gradually shaping them into the adult they will become.

Shaped by a Pacific island home… Juli reflecting as an adult

My first home, I am told, was Grand Rapids, Michigan. My parents have driven me by Butterworth Hospital where I was born and the parsonage where they first laid me down, but my first memories of home are in another place; an island in the South Pacific with 700 different tribal languages, celebration feasts of roasted pig and sweet potatoes cooked in a ground pit, mountains that kiss the clouds and dusty roads that slide into mud after a hard rain. At 18 months of age, my folks took me to Papua New Guinea, a place so distant that many were aghast that they would take a baby to such a remote place, but PNG is in my bones. It is the place from which I rise.

My parents spent their first term as Wesleyan missionaries on two different "bush" mission stations. While unusual for an American of my generation, I experienced bucket showers, outhouses, bread cooked in a woodstove and a few hours of electricity at night

provided by a generator. My babysitter spoke Wiru and Pidgin. She laughed while she sat on the back porch and watched a pack of us children coming and going from the house. We roamed about the station, fished in the pond, and played in the tall grass.

I returned to the States the year I turned from five to six. I loved being with my grandparents, visiting Santa Claus and getting occasional treats from the ice cream truck. It was a fun interlude. A place I loved to visit.

My parents' second term in PNG was in the small highland town of Mt. Hagen. There we went to school, lived in a hostel with many other Missionary Kids (MKs) who came to town to go to the government school and only visited the "bush." We vacationed on beaches and tea plantations. We swam in rivers, biked up and down our dusty road, and walked to church. The first dog I loved, Teddy, was stolen and eaten for someone's dinner. I mourned his loss especially since we had known of this possibility and kept him carefully tied up close to the house whenever we were gone.

But many more pets came. In the boarding hostel, with at times 13 children, we had turtles, guinea pigs, dogs, and cats. And our guinea pigs, dogs and cats multiplied freely. I spent hours under our house digging moats, dams and lakes with the boys. I built lakes in the road after hard rains. I chased after the moon under the shadow of banana trees and my sky contained the Southern Cross.

When I was seven, my younger brother was born. He was beautiful and he was different. My parents traveled to Australia to visit doctors. I remember sitting under my favorite tree at Tarangau School, thinking of something I had overheard. My brother "has a rare disease and an organ in his body is sending tissues up to clog his brain. He will die young." In my mind, white Kleenex was being sent up from his abdomen to stuff his brain until he died.

While this was not the case, my brother is developmentally challenged. When I was ten, my family left PNG in order for him to receive the education he needed. There is something noble in leaving home to help your brother, and I was torn by the pain in my chest that clogged my throat and loosed tears in my eyes and the hope that in America my brother could find the help he needed.

My brother did get the help he needed. He attended a school for the developmentally challenged. He learned to speak and, within a few years, my parents placed him in a small Christian school. It was a miracle for us and confirmation that we had done the right thing. But my heart still ached for home and in some ways after all these years, it still does.

The MK Adult Profile

Through research some, now adult MKs, have been given opportunity to reflect and to respond to enquiries about their childhood ecology and from these responses relevant insights have been gained. The following section outlines the responses adult MKs have had to the defining elements that have impacted their childhood development. These are tabulated (Table 3.1) as potentially positive outcomes of the MK ecology and potentially challenging outcomes.

The issues of significance can be clustered into four categories: Identity, Relationships, Mobility, and Spirituality. For the MK, the natural adolescent search for an autonomous identity can be more complicated than for the mono-cultural child. There is the negotiation of more than one country and accompanying societal demands; relationships include nurturing from alternative caregivers; mobility begins early and is sustained throughout childhood; and there is a heightened awareness of spirituality that is central to the MK ecology of development. The outcome factors listed are distinctive of the MK childhood but not unique to it. The discussion serves to highlight the distinctives of the MK developmental ecology and related adult outcomes.

The outcome factors listed are
distinctive of the MK childhood
but not unique to it.

The Identity category tabulates issues that relate to the MK's search for an answer to the questions, "Who am I?" and "Where do I belong?" In the mono-cultural context where a family retains stability of location during an individual's childhood these questions are answered by the consistency of location and the consistency of significant relationships that emerge within that stable location. In the highly mobile world of the MK, negotiating at least two countries and managing the consistent turnover of relationships that accompany such high mobility, finding satisfying answers to those questions of identity can be more of a challenge. The outcomes are profound and define the adult profile.

The Relationship category captures the MK's search for people of significance and a response to the question, "With whom do I belong?" The MK experiences relationships with a colorful array of people throughout childhood. The MK belongs within the well-defined parameters of a mission organization and is impacted by the norms and interactions within that system. The MK also interacts with nationals from the host country as well as other expatriates living in the same location. Throughout an identity search phase of life, the MK tries to determine which of these people have a reciprocal need of a relationship with him or her.

Table 3.1 Defining elements of the MK ecology and the associated potentially positive and potentially negative outcomes[1]

MK ECOLOGY	OUTCOMES	
Defining elements	Potentially positive	Potentially challenging
IDENTITY		
Negotiation of at least two countries and their respective societal demands - host country and - passport country	- Cross-cultural skills - Observational skills - Linguistic skills - Resourcefulness	- Need to control own personal world - Underdeveloped skills to be competent in passport country upon repatriation
Anticipated repatriation to a parental home country	- Value of multiculturalism	- Intolerant of even innocent mono-cultural perspectives on life
The status of being an expatriate in a host country	- Broad world view	- Confused social status
RELATIONSHIPS		
Nurturing from alternative caregivers - domestic workers - boarding house parents - other missionaries	- Tolerance and acceptance of difference	- Diminished familial bonds - Confusion over acceptable moral, cultural, and spiritual boundaries
Engagement in a sponsor agency network	- Security of system structures - Security of established social and support network	- Purposefulness of life results in tendency to make employment choices based upon service rather than academic and skill capacity; can result in long-term satisfaction or long-term challenge - Forced outward compliance to system norms; underdeveloped capacity for critical analysis and gradual development of personal choice

MK ECOLOGY	OUTCOMES	
Defining elements	Potentially positive	Potentially challenging
RELATIONSHIPS cont...		
Engagement in an expatriate community	- Inclusive relational capacity; reduced tendency to stereotype - Worldwide network of friends	- Diminished sense of belonging anywhere - High turnover of friendships
MOBILITY		
Patterns of heightened mobility	- Love of and confidence in travel - Adaptable - Self-confident	- Addiction to the "new" - Tendency towards ongoing mobility at the expense of social and career capital
Early and repeated relational loss	- Independence - Live to enjoy the present - Friendship initiation skills	- Overly self-sufficient - Unresolved grief - Relational self-protection; boundaries to relational intimacy and vulnerability
SPIRITUALITY		
The God-factor	- Early and deep awareness of the spiritual dimension of self - Benefit of early role modeling and discipleship by adults deeply committed to the Great Commission - Benefit of early exposure to global issues and opportunity to comprehend and develop a godly response	- Can feel in competition to God - Vices of passport culture taught as abstract taboos rather than experiencing gradual exposure leading to personalized commitment to honor God

The Mobility category tabulates the impact of excessive transitions experienced throughout childhood. The MK experiences the movement between at least two countries on a cyclic basis dictated by the contractual terms of his or her parents' employment. The MK is also impacted by the cyclic movement of other MKs and expatriate children living within the same location. The turnover of friendships is excessive when compared to the childhood experiences of children in mono-cultural contexts. The early and repeated relational loss has a deep and rooted impact on the adult profile of the MK.

The Spirituality category describes the impact of early and enduring awareness that God and His Great Commission is the reason for the MK life. The MK has opportunity to learn about God from an early age. The MK has opportunity to engage in dialogue with committed Christians about the Christian life from an early age. The MK has opportunity to observe the application of Christian teaching in more than one cultural context from an early age. The MK also has opportunity to be part of the cost of implementing the Great Commission from an early age. The impact is profound and the outcomes are embedded in the adult profile.

Interaction is a keyword when we examine the effects of the MK ecology. It is in dynamic processes that character is shaped. Some components of ecology are static, such as inherited characteristics. The MK inherits a disposition and is immersed in the societal expectations of a location. There is no choice in these elements of ecology. However, as time progresses and personality emerges, the MK engages more and more with elements of the ecology. Processes of change that shape character are dynamic. The things of life happen to the MK and the MK responds and reacts. The MK begins to have choices to make as to styles of interaction and in the ways to respond to elements and people who make up the developmental ecology. Over the years, the MK adopts skills that help in the negotiation of life's demands. Some adapt better than others. The length of time spent immersed in certain contexts impacts the strength of particular skills and characteristics that emerge to assist in negotiating life. Some of those skills and characteristics are helpful in adult life and some of them contribute to future challenges in lifestyle and relationships. These are the potentially positive and potentially challenging outcomes of the MK childhood ecology.

> It is in dynamic processes that
> character is shaped.

The same process of development is true for all children but emerging autonomy, establishing an independent identity, for the MK involves dealing with input from complex sources throughout developmental years. It involves a pattern of dealing with relationships that are abruptly truncated. Furthermore, it involves an early confrontation with the extremities of the Christian faith and a demand to reconcile the Great Commission with childhood developmental needs. The children of Christian families growing up mono-culturally can usually delay facing and resolving some of the complexities of identity and the cost of the call to serve God and our fellow man at least until late adolescence and early adult life but the MK begins to deal with these things early in life.

The impact is unquestionably profound.

MK relationships... Rosalea reflecting as an adult

Your mother was my first best friend, I explained to J.D. We were walking through a crowded hotel thoroughfare in Michigan, surrounded by a congestion of people who had, at various times been a part of daily life but who now were strangers, and soul-mates, with whom I crossed paths occasionally. We were together at a mission festival. J.D wanted to know how come I knew his mother and how come I knew, that she knew, the people from Papua New Guinea who walked with us. I asked J.D if his mother had ever told him her phone call story. She hadn't. I recounted for him the Christmas Eve, when my mother had told me that she thought the phone might ring very early the next morning and would I please answer it for her. It was an odd request but I was happy to agree. I always woke up early in the morning, so I would listen for the phone and answer it if it rang.

Christmas morning came and the phone rang. I jumped out of bed, remembering my responsibility.

"Hello, this is Rosalea speaking."

"Hello, this is Juli."

Juli, no, surely not. Juli had gone back to America and she wouldn't be calling because phone calls between America and Papua New Guinea were very expensive.

"Juli, is it really you? How did you get to make a phone call?"

"This is my Christmas present from my parents. I told them I wanted to phone you as my Christmas present."

When I hung up the phone, after sharing excited nothings with Juli for her allocated phone call time, I went to my room and cried. Talking on the phone was such an unfair substitute for hours spent playing together. She was 10 and I was 11; we didn't have the vocabulary to compress our lives into brief minutes of verbal exchange on a phone line. To hear her voice had been such a miracle. I'd expected never to speak to her again after she had left PNG with her family.

The day before she left PNG, we'd sat on the grass of the front lawn of the boarding hostel, in the yard where we'd spent so many inseparable hours laughing and climbing, arguing and solving the problems of our small world. We'd tried not to think about what it would be like to wake up the next day and the next and not to be able to share the hours.

Juli was my first best friend. It was awful when she left. I decided I didn't want another best friend. I'd just be friends with everyone and make sure no one was too important to me.

The phone call was your mother's only Christmas gift from your grandmother and grandfather that year, I explained to J.D. That's all she got. It was so important for us to speak to each other because we missed each other so much. It was really hard for me to go on and make other friends after she left and she had to figure out how to make friends in America.

I didn't see Juli again for almost 20 years. By then we were girls who had grown into women. I didn't think I could explain to J.D how much of a challenge it is to work through the "stuff" that makes up 20 years in order to find the girls who were once 10 and 11. He did, however, comprehend the idea of losing a friend at such a young age; he was, at the time, close enough to that age himself.

Altered perceptions…Juli reflecting as an adult

As a young child, I formed a very close friendship with the author of this book. For years after I left Papua New Guinea (PNG), when asked who my best friend was, I responded, "Rosalea." In fact, for my Christmas gift my first year in the States, I received my coveted gift, a piece of paper, at the bottom of a large wrapped box, telling me that at 3:00 pm that day I was to call Rosalea in Mt. Hagen, PNG. That was in 1977 before email and phone cards. When I called, her parents asked her to pick up the phone and she and I had a three-minute conversation.

As years progressed, I began to think that I had fabricated the closeness of that friendship. I heard of Rosalea through other MKs and occasionally through a letter (I am horrible at mail correspondence), and I began to restructure my memory. I heard how much she meant to other MKs and I began to feel that perhaps I was just one of the crowd. In devaluing this past relationship, I felt more isolated. As an adult, I can conjecture the psychological reasons why I redefined that friendship but as a young teen I did so subconsciously.

Twenty-seven years after I had left PNG, I attended a Global Mission Festival where Rosalea was also present. While walking to get dessert, I heard her tell the story of our phone conversation to my son and more importantly to share with him that even though we were so young we had shared a really important friendship. Hearing this while walking down a hotel hall brought tears to my eyes and healing to my heart. Realizing that we had mutually valued our friendship and defined it similarly gave me renewed confidence in my recalled perceptions.

With few exceptions, adult MKs will admit that a significant regret to them is the lost connection with age equivalent peers who shared their childhood ecology. The continuity of relationship with those who share childhood experiences is something to be valued and when this is sacrificed there is a significant impact on the MK.

As Table 3.1 outlines, there are many other notable adult outcomes that can be linked to the MK ecology of development. The following two chapters elaborate on each of the categories within the table and describe in further detail the adult profile of MKs.

Chapter 4: **The MK's adult profile: identity and relationships**

The significant adult outcomes of the MK ecology of development have been clustered into four major categories: Identity, Relationships, Mobility, and Spirituality. Table 3.1 details the defining elements of each category and then lists the potentially positive and potentially challenging adult outcomes that can be linked to those defining elements. The categories of identity and relationships are elaborated upon in this chapter.

Defining element of MK ecology: Identity - negotiation of at least two countries, host and passport, and their respective societal demands

Identity for the MK is shaped by location and the MK experiences of life in more than one country. The MK has a passport that links him or her to one country and a place of residence that links him or her to another country. "Who am I?" can evoke feelings of loyalty to more than one nationality. Each country is different in ethnic make-up, languages used, and economic standard. There are social norms such as standards of dress and manners of showing respect to individuals and groups of importance within each country. Each country provides a different degree of safety for the individuals living within that country. Religious composition and tolerance vary from one country to the next. The MK grows up absorbing these complexities and developing skills to negotiate the differences.

Adult outcome: Cross-cultural skills

The MK learns that there are many cultures represented in humankind and one must bridge the gaps between the cultures. The MK learns to function in a certain way with one group of people and to modify behavior when moving into the presence of a different cultural group. For example, in many social gatherings in western culture food will be served to children and young mothers first. In a rural Asian or African setting, the men and honored guests are served first and then the women and children eat later and often not in the same room as those served first. An MK learns that there are many and varied social and cultural protocols for things as mundane as the serving of food. Over time the MK adopts the posture that social norms cannot be presumed.

> Over time the MK adopts the
> posture that social norms
> cannot be presumed.

The MK develops skills of mediation. Children are more accepting of difference than adults and so they can openly explore cultural differences and help to transfer knowledge and attitudes that facilitate cross-cultural exchange. As a child the MK mixes with children of the local culture who are often more candid in explaining the intricacies of their way of life. The MK plays a role in helping expatriate adults to understand the host culture. MKs who attend schools where there are many nationalities represented in the student and teaching body hone their skills further within the daily cross-cultural encounters. Although the numerically dominant culture may dictate most terms in social interaction minority cultures are recognized and accommodated.

These skills of cross-cultural mediation are developed throughout childhood and eventually become recognizable character traits in the MK's adult profile.

<u>Adult outcome</u>: Observational skills

The power to observe, analyze, and interpret what is seen is a survival instinct for the MK. New and diverse settings are the patchwork quilt of childhood and the MK quickly learns that it is better to be equipped with information and knowledge before one acts or makes choices. Observational skills range from watching exactly how to accomplish a task that is new or foreign, to taking the time to scan a room before choosing an appropriate or expected position to assume.

MKs are often in settings where they cannot understand all of the audible communication taking place. If this is experienced habitually throughout childhood, then it is not surprising that the MK begins to rely heavily on non-verbal communication to understand interactions around him or her. Social mistakes are costly and personally painful and so throughout childhood the MK gradually becomes more expert in the skills of observation before engagement and these skills become part of the MK's adult profile.

> Social mistakes are costly and
> personally painful.

Adult outcome: Linguistic skills

Most MKs are exposed to a variety of languages. The earlier this occurs in life the more likely it is that the MK will absorb the surrounding sounds and develop capacity in more than one spoken language. Exposure to language learning, other than what is spoken in the home, during childhood enhances linguistic capacity in the adult profile.

When a child interacts on a daily basis with people who communicate in different languages, that child begins to acquire at least a conversational capacity in those languages. The child may switch easily between one language and another depending on the make-up of the group of people at a given time. Single words from one language can be borrowed while speaking another language. While this may seem strange to those with a capacity to communicate in only one language, to the MK and to those who live in multi-lingual contexts, such speech patterns are a natural dimension to communication. The exposure to such apparent communication complexities can gradually enhance the MK's linguistic skills.

Language confusion... Rosalea as a child

I got into trouble at school today. They said I was swearing. They told me not to use bad language. I'm still not sure what word was the bad word so I may get into trouble again if I accidentally say it. We were trying to get the cassette tape player to work. The Principal wanted the Australian students to hear some of the Papua New Guinea language. We were staying near my grandparents for a few months and attending the local elementary school while my parents had some leave from their mission work. My mother had a cassette tape of someone reading the story of "The three little pigs" in the Pidgin language so we'd brought that to school for the Principal to play over the loud speaker. He'd left me with some other students to set up the equipment but we couldn't get it to work.

"It's buggered up," I announced.

That's when I got into trouble.

("Bugger-up" is the Pidgin expression for "broken". It is considered coarse language in Australia. My vocabulary was littered with Pidgin expressions as well as the occasional inclusion of Huli words, the tribal language I had spoken in my early childhood.)

Adult outcome: Resourcefulness

Missionary salaries are adequate but not abundant. MKs learn early that the family budget establishes boundaries for life patterns. They learn to make do with what they have. They also develop skills to manage when the right equipment is not available. Many missionaries work in remote locations and access to services and supplies can be restricted. As MKs watch their parents adapt and cope, they also acquire skills in resourcefulness.

Adult outcome: Need to control own personal world

When the world of one's childhood has been vast enough to incorporate navigating the demands of at least two countries, one of the reactions in adulthood can be the need to be in tight control of the boundaries of one's own world. This is not necessarily in defining and controlling physical boundaries but more in terms of controlling choices and relational criteria. The MK is raised abroad because of the spiritual calling of his or her parents. Even when the MK is content or enthusiastic about the childhood experiences there is still the residual effect of having been taken into the life of an MK rather than choosing to go. The same is true for the children of other adults with highly mobile career paths so it is listed here as a distinctive factor of the MK childhood rather than a factor unique to it. The right to choose becomes important in adulthood and can be strictly guarded. The MK may avoid or resist contexts where there is a sense that freedom of choice is being inhibited.

The need to control one's personal world can impact relationships, and especially those closest to the MK. It can become the defining characteristic of relationships. A subconscious message within the MK's head might be, "As long as I am in control of things then I am not vulnerable." The control may not be through overt means but can be as subtle as withholding candid communication or levels of intimacy that help to deepen relationships and build mutual trust over time. The subconscious message may imply that "Who I am", cannot be absorbed into the collective, "Who we are" or else, once again, I am not in control of my destiny. I am not in control of my identity.

<u>Adult outcome</u>: Underdeveloped skills to be competent in passport country upon repatriation

In any country there are life skill competencies that need to be mastered. Learning to drive a car in the rural areas of Zambia will not develop the skills necessary to manage a car on the multilane expressways of Atlanta. Learning to navigate by landmarks where there are no road-signs will be a transferable skill. However, it will need some honing when the landmarks are no longer baobab trees and market stalls, but rather baseball stadiums and rest areas. An MK learns to negotiate the sensitive technicalities of country border immigration and customs but may struggle with the basic geography of his or her own passport country.

The questions, "Who am I?" and "Where do I belong?" surface and resurface as the MK wonders at the relevance of competencies developed in childhood and as the MK becomes frustrated at the needed competencies not yet mastered.

*Social competence...*Rosalea as a young adult

One hundred and twenty students sat in casual clusters about the hall. The college professor in charge of Orientation Week explained that we were to share with each other: where we were from, which football team we supported, and our star sign. My mind raced as the hum of friendly rivalry rose between students who joked about the place of their respective football teams on the competition ladder.

What was I going to say? How could I respond to any one of those three questions? Explaining where home was had already proved awkward. I couldn't really define it, even to myself. I had an Australian passport but was born in Papua New Guinea where I had, so far, lived all my life. For the past six weeks I had been living in accommodation at our denominational Bible College. I didn't feel like I was from that suburb. Conversations had already come to an abrupt end when I told enquirers that I was from Papua New Guinea. If that didn't stop them, then my response to their next question soon did. Why had I grown up there? My parents were missionaries. Being a Christian was odd enough to the average Australian, to be the child of missionaries was freakish. I had no desire to face the collective disdain of the group of college peers amongst whom I sat. (There were no Christian Liberal Arts colleges in Australia.)

Perhaps I could name a football team and try to avoid the other questions. But what if someone asked how I felt about a recent game. I would have no response. I'd arrived in Australia so recently; there had not been time to gather the needed information to competently handle this topic. And if I stumbled I'd then be back to announcing where I was from to explain my lack of knowledge.

What was the third question? It was my last chance at dignity. My star sign. I had no clue! Why would this be important introductory information anyway? Who cared? I thought star sign blurbs were just fillers for social magazines. I didn't think anyone ever took them seriously. God and PNG had formed the boundaries of my world for 18 years and I didn't have the necessary knowledge to negotiate this expansion of my world. There was so much to learn. The previous week I'd had to turn away the offer of work because I had inadvertently applied for "part-time" instead of "casual" work and so they had scheduled me on during the day when I needed to be in classes. Apparently, if you wanted evening work you had to apply for "casual." I didn't know to ask about the difference when I submitted my application.

Just this week I had been met by stunned silence when I asked a group of classmates what order the seasons came in. What does "Spring" mean if you have only ever experienced a wet and a dry season? I hadn't figured out that it would precede Summer; that Spring was the season when plants began to bloom again after the cold Winter months. One should know such basic information by the time one is 18 years of age.

My eyes darted about the room in search of the nearest exit. Perhaps I could escape to the bathroom long enough to avoid yet another uncomfortable interaction. I needed to preserve what dignity I had left if I was going to make it socially amongst this group of peers in the coming years.

Withdrawal and silence were quickly becoming my allies.

Defining element of MK ecology: Identity - anticipated repatriation to a parental home country

A defining element of the MK ecology is that life in the host country is temporary. The child's parents speak about the home country from which they have come and the MK knows that there is an expectation that at some point he or she will go and live in that country. In an instance where the parents are from two different home countries then the MK may have an option but there is usually an expectation of repatriation to a parental home country. MKs have legal permission to live in the host country as minor dependents attached to one or both parents' work permit or on student visas. The MK is there because of the parents' work. Once the parents cease to work in that country or the MK is no longer eligible for a student visa then the MK could expect to repatriate.

There are, of course, exceptions to these circumstances but generally the expectation of repatriation provides a perpetual backdrop to the accumulation of events that form the MK childhood. The MK observes while those around him or her come and go from their home countries and knows that at some point it will be his or her turn to go. Older siblings finish school and return to a parental home country to attend college or university, or to seek employment. MKs converse amongst themselves about how long they will be in the host country and when they can expect siblings to come and go. They talk about their experiences in the parents' home country and compare reactions to those experiences. They discuss whether they will finish school with their friends or not.

<u>Adult outcome</u>: Value of multiculturalism

The MK grows up valuing people and places from at least two parts of the globe. Mixing with people from multiple cultures and sharing in the habits and celebrations of at least two different cultural groups engenders in the child an appreciation of variety in cultural practices. One isolated culture can never be enough when there is a tapestry of cultures to be enjoyed. As an adult the MK seeks out other cultures and actively promotes multiculturalism. MKs surround themselves with people who also value and promote multiculturalism.

> One isolated culture can never be
> enough when there is a tapestry of
> cultures to be enjoyed.

<u>Adult outcome</u>: Intolerant of even innocent mono-cultural perspectives on life

The converse can also be true for MKs, there can be an intolerance of those who have a mono-cultural perspective on life. Such people might be regarded with disdain for their ethnocentricity. The MK can develop a superiority complex and fail to acknowledge that these individuals are merely a product of their own childhood ecology that may not have enjoyed exposure to other cultures. Where the MK automatically wonders if someone from another culture or religion would accept a given viewpoint, the individual raised with no outside exposure does not automatically initiate such enquiry.

Worldview…Rosalea reflecting as an adult

There is an amazing missions' hymn, written by a lady named Margaret Clarkson that was very popular in the conservative evangelical church during the 1970s and '80s. This was the era during which I was an MK accompanying my parents on their quadrennial visit to church congregations in Australia. My parents shared in church after church about the work of evangelism they were so deeply committed to in Papua New Guinea. Pastors and local church people were welcoming and affirming as they listened to my parents share.

My siblings and I grew very weary of hearing the same stories and sermons shared. However, the greatest irritation for me personally, was in having to sing this same hymn at each church service we attended. I was irritated by the words of the hymn and I was irritated that no-one else seemed to be irritated by the hymn. It goes like this:

> *So send I you to labor unrewarded,*
> *To serve unpaid, unloved, unsought, unknown,*
> *(But my parents do get paid a salary, and the people*
> *at Fugwa do love us and know us very well!)*
> *To bear rebuke, to suffer scorn and scoffing,*
> *(I don't remember hearing anyone speak*
> *disrespectfully to my parents for what they do!)*
> *So send I you to toil for Me alone.*

> *Refrain: As the Father hath sent me, So send I you.*
> *So send I you to bind the bruised and broken,*
> *(Okay, we help people when they are sick, and Auntie*
> *Fran runs the clinic so I guess that counts.)*
> *O'er wand'ring souls to work, to weep, to wake,*
> *To bear the burdens of a world aweary,*

So send I you to suffer for My sake.
(This song sure makes being a missionary sound like
a sad thing and I thought we loved our life!)

So send I you to loneliness and longing
(Does anyone here know how much I miss my friends
in PNG?)
With heart a-hung'ring for the loved and known
Forsaking home and kindred, friend and dear one,
(I would love to be back home again right now but
we have to visit some more churches before we can
go back to PNG.)
So send I you to know My love alone.

So send I you to leave your life's ambition,
(All my parents want to do is preach to the people of
PNG; they don't talk about anything else.)
To die to dear desire, self-will resign,
To labor long and love where men revile you,
(I guess they just don't get that the people of Fugwa
show us how much they love us.)
So send I you to lose your life in Mine.

So send I you to hearts made hard by hatred,
(Now I'm getting mad – the people of PNG don't
hate; they are kind and warm people.)
To eyes made blind because they will not see,
(When Dad preaches the people want to hear about
God.)
To spend, tho' it be blood to spend and spare not,
(Don't they get just how much we love our life and
love PNG?)
So send I you to taste of Calvary.

(I sure hope they never translate this song into Pidgin or
Huli because I never want to sing it again!)

As I reflect back now, I am conscious that I was analyzing
the words of the hymn and the sentiments on the faces of
those who sang the hymn according to my own real-
world experiences. Most of the people in the
congregations had never been outside Australia and
could only imagine the life of a missionary and the life of
people in PNG. I, on the other hand, thought about my
very real life and my very real friends each time the song
was sung and I did not nurture feelings of tolerance for

> *those who had not been privileged to experience life abroad.*
>
> *I would still choose not to sing that amazing missions' hymn again.*

Defining element of MK ecology: Identity - the status of being an expatriate in a host country

MKs know they are foreigners in the host country. Many times, they stand out because they look and speak differently to those around them, their family life patterns are different, they have different standards and ways of being educated.

There is a status that goes with being different. Sometimes the status is enviable but sometimes it can be a handicap with which to live.

There is a status that goes
with being different.

The status of being an American when the USA takes a strong stand against global terrorism can result in pain for the MK. The status of being an Australian when the Australian sportsmen are behaving disrespectfully on their overseas tours can create tension for the MK. In these instances, the MK can be looked upon as a representative of his or her passport country, a miniature ambassador and be the recipient of uninvited commentary on the choices made by genuine representatives of the country. In these instances, the status is a handicap in the MK developmental ecology.

<u>Adult outcome</u>: Broad world view

Status provides the MK with the opportunity to see the world from a broad perspective. While negotiating life between at least two countries, the MK is potentially exposed to the extremes of life as they exist economically, in social and religious observances, and in political stability or lack thereof. During childhood, the MK has repeated occasion to ask why the differences exist and what significance they have for himself or herself, and for others of a different status. This enquiry, with satisfactory answers, and the opportunity to cognitively explore issues encountered during childhood, is the making of a broad worldview. Most individuals do not face issues of social conscience or try to find personal resolution to issues such as poverty and injustice until early adulthood. The MK develops the capacity to see global and cultural issues from more than one point of view.

<u>Adult outcome</u>: Confused social status

Expatriate life can be an equalizer in terms of status. Foreigners within a given location tend to enjoy camaraderie no matter what their station in life. All are away from family and friends and value the friendships formed with other foreigners. Within international church settings the ambassador of a country holds no greater status than the humanitarian aid volunteer. MKs are raised in homes where their parents host the highest office bearers in their denomination, when they come to visit the mission work, in just the same manner in which national church workers are hosted. When a missionary family visits national church work where the adults are received as honored guests, often the MKs will be treated with the same honor. When a missionary family visits the passport country and speaks in churches to raise awareness and funds for the mission work, the MKs are received with great kindness.

However, when the MK leaves the host country and establishes autonomy apart from the family, the MK himself or herself, holds no defining status. During childhood, when mixing in the secular world, the MK is aware that he or she does not come from a wealthy family. Although honored within the church context, in the secular world the MK is just a child from a lower socio-economic family. Throughout childhood this can cause tension for the MK. It may be difficult to reconcile which status is truly representative of who he or she is in life. As an adult the MK can continue to struggle to reconcile where he or she fits socially.

Defining element of MK ecology: Relationships - Nurturing from alternative caregivers

Relationships of significance for the MK are unique. The MK is not surrounded by extended family or a consistent, homogenous social network. Usually, the MK is surrounded by people with whom his or her parents have come to serve for the fulfillment of the Great Commission. The MK is surrounded by other expatriate families who have the same purpose, within the mission agency.

In some missionary homes there are domestic workers employed to help with house and garden maintenance. Sometimes MKs are left in the care and supervision of these domestic workers. Sometimes the domestic workers bring their own children to the home and the MK can develop friendships with these children. The MK can be left in the supervision of adults from other missionary or expatriate families and relationships of significance are thereby built. In some cases, MKs attend school in locations away from where their parents work and these MKs either live in boarding home arrangements or live with families willing to accommodate them.

<u>Adult outcome</u>: Tolerance and acceptance of difference

Nurturing relationships impact a child's development. In the case of MKs, nurturing occurs from people who represent vastly different experiences in life and the MK adopts values from each of these significant people, trying to reconcile them into an independent value system and worldview. One of the outcomes of nurturing from an array of caregivers is a tolerance and acceptance of difference.

<u>Adult outcome</u>: Diminished familial bonds

Without enduring contact with extended family members throughout childhood years, the MK does not easily develop closeness with relatives in the passport country. In adult life the MK is more likely to maintain contact with families who served within the mission agency during his or her childhood than with relatives.

In the case where MKs have attended boarding school for extended periods there can also be some level of estrangement with immediate family. This is especially so when siblings have been separated for years at a time to attend school. In these instances, there are fewer shared experiences to rehearse during family gatherings and so the familial bond is less automatic. In adult life there can be greater affirmation and pleasure for the MK in getting together with close MK friends who have a catalogue of shared memories to rehearse and to build upon. There already exists a glossary of descriptive language through which the MKs can connect and communicate at a satisfying level. Mutual trust has been built over time and through enduring contact.

> There already exists a glossary of
> descriptive language through which
> the MKs can connect and
> communicate at a satisfying level.

*Extended family...*Rosalea as a child

There are two small slopes to climb between the bottom and top house on the Takaru mission station. We were standing at the top of the first incline when Wendy turned to me and told me that she was my cousin. My eyes flicked over to Ruth, my imminently wiser older sister, seeking confirmation and a clue as to what this meant. Lex, Wendy's younger brother kicked a stone, impatient to keep moving up the path. I wanted to understand what it meant to be cousins.

Martha and Ruth, my Papua New Guinean friends lived in a home down a path to our left. Their parents worked for the church in a very remote area. Martha and Ruth lived with their cousins, so they could go to the school on the Takaru mission station. But their cousins were not related to them, they just came from the same home area as Martha and Ruth's family in Papua New Guinea. Their families were loyal to each other and helped each other out when it was necessary. If Wendy and Lex were my cousins, were our families related or did we just come from the same home area in Australia? I wasn't sure.

> *Wendy saw my confusion and explained that her father was my mother's brother. We had the same grandparents. I wondered if Buddy and Karen were related to us. Their family also lived at Takaru. Were they my cousins? But their parents had come here from America when Buddy was small. And what about Auntie Delwynne? She also lived on the Takaru mission station but had come here from Australia. We all called her Aunt. Were we all related?*

<u>Adult outcome</u>: Confusion over acceptable moral, cultural, and spiritual boundaries

Exposure to a wide variety of discipline methods, culturally acceptable practices, and spiritual interpretations during childhood can result in confusion for an individual. When MKs are left under the supervision of a variety of caregivers they can experience vast differences in discipline and boundaries imposed on acceptable behavior. This is one of the major concerns of missionaries sending their children to boarding school or to be hosted in homes of others while attending school. While at home with his or her parents the child may experience firm discipline accompanied by a great deal of affection and personal attention. In a boarding arrangement there can be firm or more relaxed discipline but there is seldom as much affection and personal attention as would be experienced at home within the immediate family. Even in the most benevolent contexts the MK has to make adjustments to his or her personal needs.

Within a single mission context, it is likely that a boarding home arrangement will provide consistency in spiritual nurture for the MK. However, when the MK is left in the care of those who have alternative spiritual views there can arise some confusion. Spiritual confusion can also arise when the MK observes alternative application of spiritual principles. The principle of modesty can be applied differently in the dress code of fellow missionaries and in the standard of dress applied by nationals within the host country. Principles of biblical equality can be applied differently within the mission context, the wider church experienced within the passport country, and the national church in the host country. Observance of a wide variety of acceptable social norms in relationship with the opposite sex can lead to confusion for the MK. The MK, left under the supervision of an array of caregivers, learns to respect and care for each of them and as the years progress he or she is left to reconcile the apparent discrepancies in application of spiritual truths and socially acceptable behavior.

*Acceptable standards...*Rosalea as a child

I wanted a grass skirt. All my friends wore grass skirts and they rustled and swayed as they walked along. I really wanted a grass skirt. I wanted one that had the dark color at the bottom and the nice tight knots at the top where bunches of flattened and dried reeds were tied onto the spun-bark string. One of the older girls took me down to the swamp to show me where the reeds grew. She waded out into the murky water and pulled out a few reeds to show me how she could then take a sharpened blade made of bamboo and run it along the length of each reed to create a flattened piece of grass. We'd need a lot of reeds she told me but she said she would help me. I was willing.

We pulled and scraped until the pile of reeds was respectable. But it wasn't enough. We started again the next afternoon when my lessons were complete and her chores were done. She was a patient coach. My hands were sore and the job seemed huge, but I wanted a grass skirt.

Weeks later, after the reeds had dried and my patient friend had helped to add the color and spin the string my grass skirt was ready to wear. As I dashed into the house to try it on, so that the knot that formed the waist clasp could be tied in just the right place, my mother called. I stopped to hear her suggestion that I simply try it on, out there on the veranda. But, I didn't want to undress on the veranda and surely my mother would not approve. She thought I should leave my clothes on and simply wear the grass skirt over the top of my dress.

Why would I do that? You don't wear any other clothes with a grass skirt; it is an outfit, complete on its own. Maybe my skin was too white. Why hadn't God made me tanned like all my friends? Would it have been okay then for me to wear just the grass skirt?

Defining element of MK ecology: Relationships - Engagement in a sponsor agency network

Usually missionaries are deployed by a mission agency. There is an application process and the agency invests in the preparation of the personnel they deploy abroad. The MK belongs to a group of people and belongs within a system. These systems have norms that establish boundaries of behavior and of decision making. The system provides a network.

<u>Adult outcome</u>: Security of system structures

Structure and boundaries provide a sense of security to a child during developmental years. The MK can draw these from the mission agency. The mission agency determines contracts for the missionary family so the length of time in a host country and the length of time in the passport country is prescribed. The mission agency negotiates with personnel about acceptable provision of education for the MK; influences living standards in the host country; negotiates location of residence and job assignments for the missionary. In all of these things the MK is impacted. The system provides a structure within which the MK can predict the turns life will potentially take. The security of system structure becomes part of the MK psyche and can impact adult life choices.

<u>Adult outcome</u>: Security of established social and support network

Within the collective missionary personnel, the MK has an established social network. Even when there are tensions between missionaries, the MKs will often find friendship and support with one another. The security of this social network impacts MK development. In adult life the MK can assume and seek friendships within an employment network, finding security in these contexts.

My missionary family... Juli as a child

All the missionaries were gathered together for a biannual meeting and our little church was full of familiar faces from all the mission stations. My "family" was scattered all over the church as the children I lived with were sitting with their parents. My father, the local minister, stood up joyfully to lead the congregation in song. The song, "Jesus Laikim Olgeta" (Jesus Loves Everyone) was in the local Pidgin trade language, and equivalent in familiarity to us as "Jesus Loves Me" is to many. The song is very simple:

Jesus loves everyone,
Loves my father and my mother,
Loves my sister and my brother,
Loves you, Loves me,
Loves everyone.

As we sang together, my father belted out the song leading the festive crowd. However, in the middle of the song instead of singing:

Jesus laikim olgeta,
Laikim Papa wantaim Mama,
Bikpela susa liklik brata,
My Dad sang out:
Jesus laikim olgeta,
Laikim Papa waintaim Mama,
Bikpela susu ...

The congregation stopped singing as my father's voice petered off, everyone stared into the silence. Because instead of singing, "Jesus loves my big sister", he had sung, "Jesus loves big breasts", singing instead of susa (sister), susu (breast).

As my father's face turned red, Auntie Linda began to laugh. She laughed so hard she fell out of her chair. The rest of us joined in as contagious laughter filled the church. To this day, I am filled with the pure joy of the moment uniting us all together and still uniting me with my missionary family as I recall the connection we felt laughing together.

<u>Adult outcome</u>: Purposefulness of life results in tendency to make employment choices based upon service rather than academic and skill capacity – can result in long-term satisfaction and/or long-term challenge

Enduring engagement in the mission agency system instills within the MK purposefulness about life. Missionary families are working together abroad for a focused purpose. Research suggests that, in adult life, MKs tend to choose employment in service industries and may choose to work below their academic or skill capacity in preference to employment that allows them to help others. It seems that during childhood they absorb the value of life sacrificially given to help others whether in spiritual or humanitarian care. TCKs in general are high achievers academically and yet MKs seem to make career choices based on a purpose to serve mankind rather than on personal ambition. They can experience the satisfaction of contributing to the wellbeing of humankind in their chosen career path. However, they can also experience frustration and a lack of satisfaction if they suppress ambition and cognitive potential out of a sense of obligation to serve others. It can be a challenge to reconcile the need to make a meaningful contribution in life and the desire to be challenged in one's academic and skill capacity. This dilemma shapes the adult profile of MKs.

> MKs seem to make career choices
> based on a purpose to serve mankind
> rather than on personal ambition.

<u>Adult outcome</u>: Forced outward compliance to system norms; underdeveloped capacity for critical analysis and gradual development of personal choice

Forced compliance to system norms can serve to maintain surface level harmony within the mission network but it can also serve to disguise the gradual increase of resentment within the developing child. Mission systems can gradually develop norms about acceptable standards of discipline, acceptable dress codes, acceptable rituals and holidays to observe, acceptable manners of social interaction between children and adults, and the list goes on. Some applications of the Christian faith are simply a matter of social conscience.

Missionaries bring with them, to a shared location, differing perspectives on life. They come from different countries, they have different church backgrounds, different social interaction styles, and different value systems. There can be a lot to reconcile within the mission system network. A child can be required to comply with standards that the system imposes simply so that there is harmony, not necessarily because his or her family would otherwise adopt such norms. In such instances there can be compliance accompanied by resentment. In a less restricted environment parents may be better able to help MKs in their emerging identity search to develop critical analysis and a gradual personal choice on matters of social conscience. When compliance is forced there is less room for gradual experimentation within the confines of a safe environment.

Defining element of MK ecology: Relationships - Engagement in an expatriate community

A further network within which the MK is engaged is the expatriate community. If the MK attends school with other foreign children, there is the opportunity to develop friendships outside the mission network. Foreigners who share a location abroad often engage in social interaction. The MK is accepted and becomes part of this social network that then affects his or her development.

<u>Adult outcome</u>: Inclusive relational capacity; reduced tendency to stereotype people

The expatriate community is inclusive of people from all stations in life. Employees who hold high office within their organization are as much in need of social support and interaction as those working in more menial positions, or those who are living on locally equivalent wages. The foreigner from a fundamental religious group is as much in need of social engagement as the atheist. Within these networks of people, the MK learns that there are basic human needs and even people from vastly different walks of life can laugh and converse with one another. The MK learns to be inclusive. The MK learns that stereotyping reflects a narrowness of mind. These traits that emerge through childhood experience are embedded in the adult profile.

The MK learns to be
inclusive.

<u>Adult outcome</u>: Worldwide network of friends

The MK meets people from many different countries while living abroad. Through social engagement while abroad the MK develops friendships that will be carried on even after each person leaves the shared location. Some MKs are better at maintaining ongoing communication than others but nevertheless, they all end up with friends from around the world. In adult life there can be unexpected as well as intentional reconnections with these friends.

Truncated relationships...Rosalea reflecting as an adult

I waited for her face to come up on the screen of my laptop computer. What would she look like after all these years? I pictured in my mind the ten-year-old girl she had been and tried to construct the face of a woman of 40 years out of that image. Somehow, I couldn't put the light brown hair, the pony tail, and the trade mark freckles on an adult woman's face. I knew she would not be tall, we'd both been below average height even in elementary school.

For five years we had been trying to reconnect. I had tracked down her parents when I began my academic research, through an organization that facilitated ongoing connection between retired Australian government representatives who had worked in Papua New Guinea during its brief and mandated colonization. Her mother, kind and pleasant to me as a child, was only too happy to fill me in on the achievements and life journey of her daughter, who had been my friend. We almost managed to meet up in Australia five years ago but the plans had to be suddenly cancelled. Two or three times in the ensuing years we had e-mailed hoping to cross paths on one of the three continents we had in common. She lived and worked in the USA and I made occasional visits there, but the timing was never right. I lived and worked in Africa and she made occasional visits there, but her visits had so far never been to the southern tip of the vast continent, where I lived. Earlier in the year each of our fathers had fallen seriously ill and we'd each traveled home to Australia but we missed again by weeks.

Now she was coming to stay in my home for two nights. Work had brought her to southern Africa and she wanted to know if we could reconnect. I invited her to my home and she accepted. I was to pick her up at the airport and we would spend a day together at a game reserve, enjoying the viewing of big game in their natural habitat. We hosted many visitors in our home and we often took them to see the African animals. Africa was a long way from the mountainous Pacific island of our childhood. Those childhood years had been more than 30 years ago. How would we recognize each other?

Her face came up on the screen and I smiled as I thought of the carefree play of those childhood days and imagined the essence of the same person inside the image of the person who was now a woman. I wondered if she had tried to construct a grown woman's face from the freckled face and bleach white hair that had been my childhood image. The exchange of photos would help us to recognize each other at the airport. She would be another guest whom I would enjoy, except this one had been my friend for a short but significant season during my child-life.

<u>Adult outcome</u>: Diminished sense of belonging anywhere

When friendships of significance are drawn from all over the globe the MK can experience a diminished sense of belonging to any one place. The passport that the MK holds is a legal right to live and function within a given country. However, if all social and developmental experiences of significance have occurred in another country or with a group of peers from yet a third country, then there can be a diminished sense of belonging. In adult life this can continue to affect the MK, who may have a reluctant loyalty to any country of residence.

Leaving home…Juli reflecting as an adult

I recall, with tears in my eyes almost 30 years later, the desperate fear that came when I left home at the age of ten – leaving my homeland and my people. My people were the other MKs, the other international kids who attended my school, my aunts and uncles (the other adult missionaries) and the New Guinean people. My home was full of rushing wild rivers, full of boulders with sandy beaches here and there. My home was mountainous, the valleys twined between ranges, towns or villages always nestled. My people were from everywhere. And I did not want to leave my everywhere. My town with racket ball courts, two or three restaurants, markets with peanuts, lemons and sweet potatoes, China "town" where we ate salty plums and visited Auntie Sylvia at the Christian bookstore. My ten-year-old body shook with sadness; tears wet my checkered dress as I watched the island of New Guinea finally disappear behind the clouds. I knew we would not return because my younger brother needed special education, and I knew that my world would change dramatically. What I did not expect was that I was to enter a world in which this experience had no relevance. A world where, who I had been, and who I currently was had no place.

<u>Adult outcome</u>: High turnover of friendships

Friendships with people within the mission agency and within the expatriate community necessarily result in a high turnover of friendships. Each foreign deployed family is on a different contractual cycle and so friends come and go all the time within each network of friends. Even with friendships drawn from the host country, there can be a turnover of friendships as the MK comes and goes. During the periods of absence, the national friends move on with their lives and develop deeper connections with those more stable in the community. This high turnover of friendships can become habitual to the MK who continues the pattern of beginning and ending friendships in adult life.

Within the MK developmental ecology issues that relate to identity and relationship must be resolved and negotiated. The outcomes clustered within these two categories can be potentially positive and potentially challenging in adult life. In the following chapter the elaboration on the adult outcomes of the MK developmental ecology is continued as the third and fourth categories are discussed: mobility and spirituality.

Chapter 5: **The MK's adult profile: mobility and spirituality**

Defining element of MK ecology: Mobility - Patterns of heightened mobility

MKs move a great deal during childhood. They spend years living within a host country and then they move to their passport country for briefer periods so that their parents can raise awareness and funds for their missionary work. MKs may travel with their parents while spending time in the passport country. Sometimes MKs will return with their parents to the same location in the host country when they are redeployed abroad but sometimes parents are reassigned to a new location and MKs experience another move. MKs who live away from home to attend school will move between home and school regularly throughout the year. Mobility is a way of life during season abroad for the MK and it impacts development.

<u>Adult outcome</u>: Love of and confidence in travel

Typically, MKs become confident travelers from a young age. They learn the vocabulary and protocol for negotiating immigration and customs at country borders. They learn the value of a passport and a valid visa. They learn to read the body language of border control personnel and they learn to communicate efficiently with airline personnel. From childhood, MKs learn to love travel and they become confident in international travel as a significant part of life. This confidence only increases as they become older.

There are, of course, exceptions to those who love to travel. A minority of MKs choose not to travel at all in adult life, having experienced as much as they care for during childhood. However, if they needed to travel in adult life, they would certainly share the confidence carried by those for whom travel is an ongoing passion in adult life.

Adult outcome: Adaptable

Heightened mobility demands adaptability. The MK learns to accommodate change and learns to adapt to meet changing demands. Unexpected changes and demands can be stressful for some people, but research suggests that MKs qualify themselves as very adaptable people.

Adult outcome: Self-confident

MKs develop self-confidence as they face the many changes experienced during childhood. Obviously, this is not the universal experience of MKs, but research findings confirm that MKs describe self-confidence as one of the strongest outcomes of their childhood experiences. They are required to manage new experiences consistently throughout childhood and thereby develop a belief in their own competence.

Adult outcome: Addiction to the "new"

Constant change resulting from heightened mobility in childhood can result in an addiction to new experiences. The MK, in adult life can be regularly looking for new things to try and new challenges to overcome. The adult MK can readily become bored with the routine of life once the challenges have been mastered and the novelty of an experience has worn off. The MK may be impatient to move on to new experiences fearing that there will not be enough time in life to experience all that there is to see and do. There may be a sense of unease or discomfort with a routine life that does not offer the potential to explore new experiences. Those close to an adult MK may find this challenging to understand. However, it is an adult profile trait that results from the childhood ecology with its breadth and constancy of new experiences.

> The adult MK can readily become bored
> with the routine of life once the challenges
> have been mastered and the novelty of an
> experience has worn off.

<u>Adult outcome</u>: Tendency towards ongoing mobility at the expense of social and career capital

In searching for new experiences and new places to see, the adult MK can develop a tendency towards ongoing mobility in adult life. The highly mobile childhood has become an adult life pattern. Sometimes such tendencies can be satisfied by the choice of a career that affords ongoing mobility. However, many times this means that the MK will choose to move regularly as an adult, changing jobs and changing social networks. This can be at the cost of promotion opportunities that come with longevity and experience within a company. This can also be at the cost of social stability. If the adult MK is married and has children, then these adult life choices have a significant impact on the family members.

Defining element of MK ecology: Mobility - Early and repeated relational loss

Heightened mobility during childhood necessarily means that the MK is confronted with relational loss from an early age. The MK who is born in his or her passport country and then moves abroad, leaves behind family and friends. Throughout childhood the high turnover of friends experienced means that the pattern of relational loss is an enduring pattern. This pattern impacts childhood development.

> The pattern of relational loss
> is an enduring pattern.

<u>Adult outcome</u>: Independence

MKs learn to be very independent. They learn to be self-reliant in many areas of their lives because they do not have a consistent network of friends upon which to lean. They learn to do things on their own because close friends are not always accessible.

Adult outcome: Live to enjoy the present

MKs quickly learn to make the most of what time they have with people and in places that are significant to them. When friends come and go and when places of residence keep changing, the MK learns that every moment is to be enjoyed simply for what it presents.

Adult outcome: Friendship initiation skills

MKs are constantly entering social networks and therefore have to develop skills for making friends. This is not always easy and often comes at high cost to the MK, but they do learn to engage new acquaintances in conversation and establish common interests in order to initiate dialogue. Even when MKs leave a place of residence for a period of time and return to it, they often find that there are new people within the location and new friendships need to be initiated so friendship initiating skills become a part of an essential repertoire of competencies. These become embedded over time and adult MKs are so equipped in adult life.

Adult outcome: Overly self-sufficient

The MK who has experienced high mobility in childhood becomes overly self-sufficient. It can become difficult to let people help. During childhood there may not always be people around to offer support and assistance so the MK learns to manage alone. The childhood habit becomes an adult trait.

The MK learns to
manage alone.

Adult outcome: Unresolved grief

Not many people are well equipped for grieving when loss is first experienced. Missionary parents are not trained in how to help their children resolve grief experienced from leave-taking. Boarding house parents are not trained in grief-management so cannot help MKs process their grief. Therefore, MKs absorb loss and pain in whatever way comes naturally to their personality. Some suppress their feelings; some overreact to the pain of loss and act out in physical or emotional responses. Whatever the response, MKs usually carry into adult life unresolved grief. Furthermore, they carry into adult life well developed patterns of responding to grief and these patterns are not always healthy; they can impact adult relationships subsequently experienced by the MK.

<u>Adult outcome</u>: Relational self-protection; boundaries to relational intimacy and vulnerability

The pain of losing friends and separation from family members causes MKs to sub-consciously develop systems of self-protection against such pain. Deeper vulnerability and deeper intimacy result in deeper pain when separation eventuates. Therefore, the MK sub-consciously rationalizes that if he or she is in control of the depth of vulnerability and intimacy then he or she will also be in control of the depth of eventual pain resulting from separation. For some MKs this self-protection is through careful management or withholding the sharing of sincere feelings on issues of importance. For some it is careful management or withholding of physical contact. For some it is careful management or withholding of time. Relational self-protection is embedded in the adult MK make-up and it can be directly linked to experiences during childhood years.

*Systems of self-protection...*Rosalea as a child

The sobbing gradually gave way to the heavy breathing of exhausted sleep. I crawled back into my own bed and lay staring at the ceiling, wondering how many more nights the pain of separation from her mother would cause my young boarding home sister to sob herself to sleep. At 10 years of age I longed for the reassurance of my own mother. We all missed our families. Bedtime was the worst for some, especially those who were accustomed to expressions of affection and intimate dialogue at that time of the day. I missed my mother at the end of the school day when I wanted to share about the people and events of the day while I had been out of the home. No one watches you like your own mother and no one cares about the details of life as much as your own mother.

I had no words to describe my empathy so I sat beside her night after night so she could see that I was there while she fell asleep. When she first came to the boarding home I would walk down the corridor and through the dining and living rooms in search of our boarding home mother when I heard the sobbing. Now I just sat beside her and waited for sleep to come to her. The confusion and longing was heard in each sob. Sometimes I would reach out to touch her but touch was hard for me. Touch conveys too much and makes you vulnerable. I was afraid to show my feelings in case my own confusion took over and I ended up crying with her.

The other two young girls in my room would lie silent, helpless to alleviate the pain. One carried her own pain stoically and I often had to remind myself to take the time to draw out her expressions of emotion. The other masked her pain with a disciplined routine. We'd been together for some months and had a comfortable understanding. None of us could explain to our new boarding home sister that the pain would eventually subside and only emerge in occasional surges. Some of us needed space and isolation during those surges. Some needed the reassurance of physical touch. Sport and aggression helped others. We recognized the need in each other and tried to support as best we could.

Being seen, being present and accessible, seemed important to our new boarding home sister. She followed me around at school, keeping me in sight even when she couldn't participate in my activities. Our teachers compassionately accommodated her needs in the early days when she refused to remain in her own room and preferred to sit with me in a class with students five years her senior. Now she just waited for me to come out of my classroom at break time.

Still staring at the ceiling, I wished my birth sister was here. She'd been the oldest girl in the boarding home last year and sometimes I didn't have to be the one to try to figure out what the younger ones needed. She started high school this year and had to move to another town. During the next school break, back with my own family, I could enjoy the luxury of being the youngest child. For now, my role was to reassure my boarding home sisters that I remained accessible even when I was out of their sight.

Defining element of MK ecology: Spirituality—The God-factor[1]

God is the central factor in the life of the MK throughout childhood. Most MKs receive consistent teaching from the Bible. Most experiences of life are referenced by God's character and His plan for mankind. God and His Word is the backdrop upon which the MK life is painted. No honest reflection on the MK developmental ecology is complete without an acknowledgement that God is the central factor in the MK's emerging identity.

> God is the central factor in the life of
> the MK throughout childhood.

<u>Adult outcome</u>: Early and deep awareness of the spiritual dimension of self

Missionaries are people who have expressed a specific calling to serve God. They are people who have been willing to sacrifice a life in the home country for the sake of helping to achieve the Great Commission. Missionaries typically have a deep and well-grounded understanding of the spiritual dimension of self and they seek to convey this to their children as they grow.

MKs sometimes have the opportunity to see alternative spiritual forces in action. Where missionaries are placed among people who are overtly against Christianity and the authority of God there can be manifestations of evil forces at work and the MK may be exposed to these spiritual realms. An awareness of the reality of spiritual forces remains with the MK into adult life.

Childhood experiences that relate to spiritual forces can result in extreme confusion for the MK. Sometimes this confusion is resolved and sometimes it is not.

Safety and spirituality…Juli reflecting as an adult

As a young MK, I was sexually abused by two different expatriate perpetrators while my family was in our host country. The trauma, which I kept as a secret, impacted not only my concept of self and safety but also my concept of God and service. As a child and teen, I heard repeated recollections from my parents of God's promise to protect their children. My family returned to the States, and my parents traveled to many churches sharing the powerful stories that reflected God's ongoing faithfulness to this promise. My brother was repeatedly and miraculously saved from death. My father's thumb was basically cut off, and while being saddled with an uncooperative pilot who refused to take him to the best regional hospital, he arrived despairingly at a small clinic that for only a few weeks was being serviced by a prestigious hand surgeon. This story stirs in me, even now, awe at God's ongoing providence. Yet, I had repeatedly been sexually molested by the age of seven. God had not protected me and as a young adult in therapy, I felt angry, suicidal and betrayed by the very God who had answered so many of my prayers.

As a young child growing up in a culture where the spirit world is an acknowledged reality, I learned to know that Jesus' name keeps me safe from any evil spirits. Never once has this belief faltered. As a young child, I prayed for rain in a time of drought, and as I said "Amen" the drops began to fall. As a young child, I saw the love my parents had for the people to whom they were called to live amongst. I remember a mentally unstable woman who danced naked and loudly in the middle of the road while others stood and laughed, and yet when she came over to our vehicle and wanted to touch my hair, my mother held me close and encouraged me to let her. And this crazed woman reached out and so gently touched my young head.

Once, as a young child, I disparagingly said the word "native" to my father repeating something I had overheard. He immediately stopped walking and informed me that I too was a native of America and that we are all natives of somewhere and to never speak badly about someone because of where they are from or the color of their skin. This brief lesson at the age of four has shaped my entire life dramatically. God has molded and gifted me out of my TCK experiences. Yet, I was not kept safe from predators and this lack of safety for a long while impacted my ability to put my full trust in God, my Creator. I have also heard from many friends, other MKs, who have had a variety of traumatic experiences while their parents were overseas.

I still don't have an answer to why these hurtful experiences occur when the faithful respond to God's call. This theological question has rattled around in my head for a long time. I have read books, knelt in prayer, yelled or raged against the Almighty, yet what I have found is that God has never stopped calling me to Himself. As I have matured, I have realized that in being called again and again into relationship with God to be a follower of Jesus Christ, God's promise given to my parents, years ago is fulfilled. God promised to keep me safe when my parents took off to a remote mission with an 18-month-old girl, and while in this lifetime I was not kept safe, in the next I will be in the safest place of all.

<u>Adult outcome</u>: Benefit of early role modeling and discipleship by adults deeply committed to the Great Commission

MKs grow-up surrounded by people committed to serving God, to the point of sacrifice. They know why they are living abroad. They watch while their parents and other missionaries work to help people understand God and grow in their relationship with Him. As the MK grows older non-familial adults begin to have a greater significance in the development of the child and so the input from other adults who take time to intentionally disciple the MK is significant. Sincere discipleship impacts life choices made by the MK and so affects the adult profile.

The practice of tithing... Rosalea as a child

I played with the two silver coins in my pocket as I stepped carefully around the mounds of sweet potato, tomatoes, and the leafy bunches of silver-beet. I hoped Uncle Don would walk past the cabbage today so that we wouldn't have sauerkraut on this week's menu at the boarding hostel. The women sitting on the ground behind the mounds of fresh vegetables at the Mt. Hagen market never failed to shake their heads and click their fingernails against their teeth as we traipsed by on our weekly Saturday morning shopping trips.

We girls loved to go to the market with Uncle Don and carry the locally made string bags he brought with him to transport all the fruit and vegetables he bought for the meals we would have in the coming week. The local women would ask him how many wives he had because there were so many of us and we were all of a similar age. Some of us had blonde, almost white hair, and pasty colored skin; some had very black hair and olive colored skin. He must have many wives, they concluded. Uncle Don would laugh and tell them he had only one wife but we were all his daughters. He treated us all as though we were his own and we loved him for it.

Our parents worked in rural areas and we lived with Uncle Don and Auntie Joy in a big home, along with some of the boys from our mission families. We attended the local international school where we blended in amongst the many nationalities represented. But, at the market, we didn't blend in. We arrived in a big green bus from which we happily tumbled out each Saturday morning, to follow Uncle Don single-file around the market for a half an hour. We had to step carefully, single-file because the fresh produce was arranged in rows with the owners of the fruit and vegetables sitting behind each arrangement.

My silver coins grew slippery as my fingers spun them over and over in my pocket. What would I buy today when we stopped at the shops in town on the way home? My favorite choice was the bag of sweet but tangy dried and salted plums we could buy at the Chinese store. They'd begun to sell some larger sized salty plums and they were sweeter than the small ones we had grown to enjoy. Salty plums were a treat that lasted the whole day because you could suck them and suck them till they were dry. You could share them with a friend while you lay on the grass in the back yard of the boarding hostel or made up a play with whoever wanted to join you in one of the bigger bedrooms. Or, I could buy a bag of doughnuts. You could get three cinnamon and sugar-coated doughnuts in exchange for the two coins I had in my pocket. But that was only a moment of pleasure beside the salty plums. Some of the girls liked to buy a bottle of Coke™ with their weekly allowance but I had not acquired a taste for the drink, which I didn't yet know was universally sold. Sometimes, at home with my family, my Dad would buy a crate of Fanta™ bottles as a treat or for a special occasion.

Today I would buy a bag of the big salty plums. Maybe Uncle Don would take us swimming in the Kum River later in the afternoon and I could share my salty plums with the others on the bus ride to the river. I thought about the third silver coin that I had safely stored in the purse on my bedside table. That was for the offering plate in church tomorrow. We girls held each other accountable for putting our tithe in the plate each Sunday. No one brought that third coin to the market or to town on our Saturday morning outings. Once placed in our hands it went straight to our special places of safekeeping because it was only trusted to us for a short time and then we were to give it back to God.

It was not until many years later that I realized we had faithfully been giving God 33% of our weekly income but by then the concept of tithing, of faithfully giving back to God, was deeply embedded in the psyche of every one of the girls who formed that single-file chain behind Uncle Don each Saturday morning. Giving to God has never been a challenge.

<u>Adult outcome</u>: Benefit of early exposure to global issues and opportunity to comprehend and develop a godly response

Global issues such as poverty and injustice are naturally seen by the MK through the filter of the God-factor. The questions of why God allows injustice in the world, why does He not intervene on behalf of the oppressed and impoverished, and why some nations seem to succeed while others experience perpetual struggle are an automatic response to the extremes of human life witnessed while the MK travels. From earliest years the MK tries to reconcile the pain in the world with the loving God of creation who is depicted in the consistent Christian discipleship he or she is privileged to experience. The MK who is allowed to cognitively and experientially explore these significant issues and come to a conclusion that is credible to himself or herself at the specific stage of development he or she has reached, will succeed in reconciling a godly response to these global issues. The MK who is handed canned or prescribed responses to these significant issues will early begin to question the authenticity of God. The God-factor is central to the existence of the MK and if God is perceived as contradictory, shallow, or insincere then this will impact the adult profile of the MK. If, however, God is perceived as approachable, fair, and One who has a plan to respond to the extremes of life, then this will impact the MK adult profile in an alternative outcome.

> Global issues such as poverty and injustice
> are naturally seen by the MK through the
> filter of the God-factor.

<u>Adult outcome</u>: Can feel in competition to God

If God does not seem to have a reasonable plan for the world, and seems not to be willing to intervene on behalf of the hurting, then the MK will struggle to believe that God is concerned about his or her own needs either. Where difficult family choices have to be made to cater for schooling and social development of missionary children the MK may feel that God and the non-Christian people of the host country are more important to his or her parents than the MK himself or herself. The MK may feel that more focused nurturing was needed during developmental years and he or she had to compete with God in order to get the attention of his or her parents. God is a formidable opponent in such a challenge. The outcome can be resentment and a mistrust of God in adult life.

God is a formidable opponent
in such a challenge.

Alternatively, the MK may determine that God has trusted him or her from an early age to be part of the Great Commission. The MK may develop a comprehensive God concept through the experience. Even if this is the case, the MK may still have to accommodate some residual effects of having felt in competition with God for parental attention and nurture during childhood.

<u>Adult outcome</u>: Vices of passport culture taught as abstract taboos rather than experiencing gradual exposure leading to personalized commitment to honor God

Although the MK is exposed to global issues during childhood, he or she may not experience gradual exposure to negative behavior and vices common to the passport culture. Practical Christianity for the MK involves sharing about God's teachings, a life of service to mankind, and maintaining the mission agency norms. At the same time missionary parents try to teach their children about the evils of such things as drunkenness and promiscuity as they might be manifested in the passport country. Rules and guidelines of behavior are taught as abstract concepts if there is no opportunity for gradual exposure to these vices.

In such a context it is difficult for the MK to personalize a commitment to honor God through pure living as it might be represented in the passport country. Therefore, when the MK takes up residence in the passport country and a favorite relative is found to indulge in one such vice while at the same time professing a deep love of God, it can be a very confusing time for the MK. The seemingly well-developed understanding of God can be questioned. Or, the MK can assume a legalistic, morally superior stance.

In research, adult MKs report that reconciling the God-factor to attain a personalized, relevant, context-appropriate life of Christian holiness can be a challenge.

Am I competing with God?...Rosalea as a child

The boarding hostel was a fun place to live. There were always enough kids in the yard to get a game of just about anything going. All our parents lived in outlying rural areas of Papua New Guinea working toward the mission goals of evangelization, pastoral training, and projects of development in education and medicine. We went home during the school holidays but during the term we missionary children lived together in a big home with one of the missionary families, assigned to the role of caring for and nurturing us. Every day we loaded into a big green bus and drove across town to the international school where we each attended our classes. At the end of the day one of the hostel parents would collect us from school and we would come home to a snack, piano practice, and games in the back yard.

It was girls against boys at badminton that afternoon. I was enjoying the energy and competition but we were not winning. The shuttlecock went back and forth and we laughed and dived trying to keep it in the air. Then, it landed on the roof. No matter, we often had to retrieve it from the roof. But I wanted to win! Steve had taken off for the side of the house. Steve was three years younger than me and I figured I could beat him to the shuttlecock. I clambered up the wooden tank stand and then braced myself between the two aluminum water tanks that collected rainwater for our home, shimmying up from rung to rung. Urging myself on, I kept an eye on Steve's pace. He'd had a head start on me so I had to take a shortcut across the plastic roofing to get to the shuttlecock first. I stepped across one beam, glanced over to see where Steve was and placed my feet down again ....

I woke up with my head on a soft pillow and tried to move my arms and feet. My body ached as I slowly lifted my hands above the blanket and rolled onto my side. I was sore all over. I called out for my mother and Auntie Joy came into the room looking very worried.

The corrugated Perspex sheets that formed a sunroof on the veranda had cracked when I had misplaced my feet. I'd fallen right through the roofing, landing on the wooden decking below, narrowly missing the cast iron stove we used to heat water for our baths. I'd been knocked unconscious. Uncle Don had been called for and he'd come hurrying from the church around the corner. Should they move me or not? Was my back broken? No one knew. And then I moved. I'd been carried to the car and taken to the hospital for examination. Apparently, there was no permanent damage only severe bruising. I wanted my mother.

Joy fussed and Don joked as they cared for me. My hostel siblings sat on my bed telling me about the happenings at school each day and encouraging me to sit up and try to participate in games. I wanted my mother.

A package arrived with cards and hand-made games from my friends and teacher at school. They said they missed me and wanted me to hurry back to school. The bruising was healing and I was moving around more at the hostel. I'd go back to school soon. A package arrived in the mail. I opened the card and smiled at the magazine cut out of a tube of Savlon™. I'd joked with my mother during the last school holidays that she believed Savlon™ (an antiseptic cream) fixed everything. My mother had lovingly searched through magazines and found jokes and clever sayings to make a booklet that told me how much she cared about me and how well she knew me. She knew I would be hurting. Under the card lay an apple green colored housecoat she had made. I lifted it up and noticed that each seam had been hand stitched. As I read the accompanying letter I learned that my mother had been on an evangelistic trip with my father around the villages that surrounded the Bible School where they taught. She'd been teaching and discipling people as they traveled and while sitting under the trees, talking to the women during the day, she had hand stitched the housecoat for me. It was an expression of her love.

I wanted my mother but she hadn't come. She had wanted to come and she had found a way to communicate her care for me and her knowledge of my pain. But she hadn't come. I was nine years old and I was trying to understand why God would want me to be away from my mother when I was hurting so much. I knew God was the reason we children lived away from home and I was okay with that. I loved God and I was beginning to understand that there was more peace in living the way He asked us to, than in trying to figure things out for myself. But this one was big. My pain was big. I wanted my mother and I felt like I was competing with God for her time and attention. That was too hard to understand.

Many years later, I have looked back and processed that incident in my childhood. The pain is still there. I love God more deeply and I still value the nurture and care of my mother. I will quickly run to the defense of my mother for the choice she made at that time, but I will quickly speak up in my own defense for the legitimacy of the pain and the questioning at that time. My mother will tell you that God gave her an "Abraham" experience with each of her children. Could it be that God gave me the "Isaac" experience? I'm convinced that Isaac was also asked by God whether he trusted God enough to provide and protect. I'm equally convinced that there was residual pain for both Abraham and Isaac.

Totally trusting God... Dorothy as a missionary mother

"Rosalea is in hospital and will be staying there overnight, but she's okay, she's fine." This was the message that had just come over the two-way radio to us at the rural mission compound. Rosalea, our nine-year-old daughter, was living in our boarding hostel and attending school in Mt. Hagen, while my husband, Walter and I were teaching in the mission Bible School. She had climbed onto the roof to get a badminton shuttlecock then had fallen through the Perspex onto the wooden veranda floor, and was knocked unconscious by the impact of the fall.

My first thought was, "I want to go to Mt. Hagen to be with her". Then the practicalities presented themselves. It was late afternoon. Our mission had two 15-minute allotted or scheduled times (sked times) on the two-way radio frequencies and these were at 9:30 am and 4:15 pm, during which times we were able to relay messages to one another at our various locations of ministry. This message had come during our afternoon sked time. From where I was to Mt. Hagen it was a four-hour drive in the best circumstances, and the first hour was one that I had never driven myself, over a treacherous mountain track. It would be well after hospital visiting hours when I, and whomever I could persuade to take me, would arrive. A night drive was just not practicable. The other consideration was that early the next morning we had planned to leave with a team of Bible School students for an outlying village, where the students had been deployed to do the practical part of their evangelism course. The class had been divided into three teams and Walter and I had planned to visit each team during the following week and see how each student was doing.

Finally, after signing off on the sked and bidding farewell to the other missionaries who had come to listen, Walter and I had some time alone. We talked and prayed. Walter pointed out that we had been assured that Rosalea was okay, she was fine. Eventually, after telling God what I wanted, I began to listen to Him. God spoke to me in my heart. He pointed out that we had dedicated Rosalea to Him. When we had to send her to board at the hostel, we had again asked God to care for her, as we did each day for all our children. I'm sure God had His tongue in His cheek when he spoke to me next, asking me if I didn't think He had done a good job so far? Then He asked me if I didn't trust Him for the next 24 hours, and the following week and forever?

I still needed that last bit of assurance, so I asked Walter if, instead of leaving at 6 am as planned, we could wait until after the MAF (Mission Aviation Fellowship) sked time at 7:15 am, when I would try to contact others in Mt. Hagen who might be able to give me an updated medical report on Rosalea. MAF facilitated such information for those in outlying areas since they were often called upon to fly missionaries in and out of isolated areas in the case of emergencies. Of course, the report was that she was fine. She had been discharged the previous evening, and apart from a headache, everything was okay.

The hardest thing that I, as a missionary mother had to do was to send each of our children off to board because of schooling. I had a separate experience where God challenged me on my willingness to give each one into His care. One challenge was from the Scriptures, Matthew 10:37 "Anyone who loves his father or mother more than me is not worthy of me; anyone who loves his son or daughter more than me is not worthy of me" (NIV). God used different methods of communicating with me, but always on the same theme as regards my children, "Do you truly love me more than these?" John 21:15b (NIV). I had to learn to totally trust God in all things. I am so prone to want my way.

In the next chapter we begin to look at the unique factors of significance that make up the MK ecology. Although the details vary, these factors of significance can be found in the broader experience of most MKs no matter the physical location of their childhood. The ecology is made up of experiences that any MK recognizes as familiar.

Part 2: Why they are who they are

Chapter 6: **The developmental ecology shapes the MK**

The MK Ecology

Earlier in the book the distinction was drawn between environment and ecology. To understand why the adult MK manifests the profile traits described in the preceding chapters it is necessary to explore in depth the dynamics of the MK developmental ecology. What are the forces at work in the experiences that are common to almost every MK childhood that ultimately lead to the adult profile?

A developmental ecology is the context in which a child grows up. Ecology includes the environment but incorporates much more than just the static elements that surround the child. It incorporates all the events of childhood and the relationships between the people who are encountered during those years. The ecology includes the way people relate to the child and the way the child responds or reacts to those people and to the events that are experienced. Ecology is the comprehensive experience of childhood. The child is born with a disposition, but that disposition emerges into a personality as it is shaped by the surrounding experiences. People relate to the child and the child responds, at first automatically, but as a personal identity begins to emerge then there are choices made as to how to respond.

Timing is an important element of the developmental ecology. Timing includes an accumulation of events. Over time events build up and gradually shape the child. An example of this is the experience of heightened mobility. One move impacts the child, changing schools nine times dramatically impacts the child's development. Timing also refers to the point at which things happen in the child's development. It is in these dynamic processes that character is shaped.

Self

At the center of the MK ecology is Self, the child himself or herself. DNA dictates the child's predisposition including the relative strength of extroversion, openness, neuroticism, conscientiousness, and agreeableness. Research conducted with twins separated at birth and reared apart suggests that inherited qualities account for approximately 45% of the total adult personality. The remaining 55% is influenced by the environment of one's childhood. Therefore, Self is a significant element of the developmental ecology.[1]

It could be that extreme environments impact more heavily on the development of the child. MK childhood development takes place between at least two contrasting cultures and involves a heightened degree of mobility and a heightened turnover of friendships so it could be regarded as an extreme environment. In such an instance environment may have a stronger impact on child development. However, for the sake of this discussion, it is a reliable estimate that approximately half of the adult personality profile that an individual manifests is inherited biologically and the other half is shaped by environment.

In Figure 6.1, the shaded circle around the letter "A" represents Self at the center of the MK developmental ecology. No matter where the child lives or with whom the child lives Self represents the inherited parts of the ecology. Self is part of the ecology, in fact central to the ecology.

Figure 6.1 The concentric circle representation of a child's developmental ecology. Self is represented as the central circle "A".

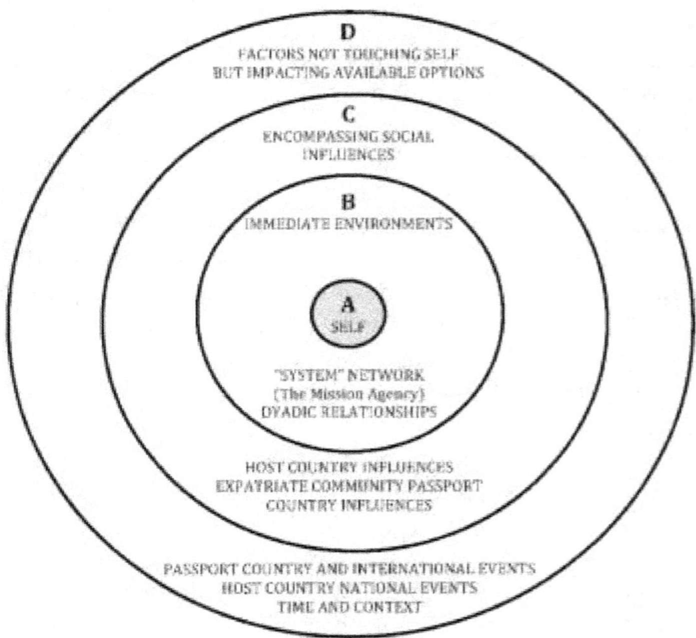

Each child is born with a unique DNA structure. Even children born from the same biological parents have a unique DNA structure. There may be striking similarities in looks, mannerisms, and behaviors but no two children are entirely identical. In fact, within families there can be stark contrasts between siblings. For each sibling, Self represents the unique inherited traits.

The influence of Self as an agent, a significant element, within the developmental ecology accounts for the fact that MK siblings can share all the same experiences throughout childhood and yet each experience different stresses along the way. For example, one child within a family may be an extreme extrovert while his or her sibling is introverted. DNA has determined the distribution of this particular trait. When MKs are called upon to mix excessively with church supporters while the family travels around the passport country raising awareness and funds for the mission work one child may thrive in the social opportunities while the second child may experience considerable stress. Conversely, if they return to a host country culture where children are expected to remain in the background and not express their opinions openly, then the stress level will increase for the extroverted child and drop for the introverted child, at least in this area of development. However, there will be heightened stress on both children if they move back and forth between the two contexts on a regular basis. They will each be expected to manifest natural tendencies in the one context and suppress natural tendencies in the other context. All children are expected to manage their natural tendencies to fit within social norms. However, the MK ecology presents extreme contexts to comprehend and accommodate while the child is developing.

> All children are expected to
> manage their natural tendencies
> to fit within social norms.

Another example may be with predispositions towards neuroticism. This too, is an inherited tendency, determined biologically by DNA. Neuroticism is the inclination to worry or become anxious. MKs who inherit minimal neurotic tendencies in their personality make-up may find the constant changes of the MK lifestyle of little concern. However, those with heightened neurotic tendencies may find many details to be anxious about in the regular demands to adapt to new situations. Two siblings experiencing the same lifestyle can respond in completely contrasting manners. In such a context there may be a heightened bond between the two siblings as one relies heavily for reassurance on the other and the second assumes the role of protector over the more anxious child. In this instance, Self has impacted the outcome for both siblings. It is likely that in adult life there will be an ongoing bond between the two siblings based upon the childhood experiences. The inherited traits of Self, together with the demands of the overall ecology, have determined this outcome.

In the early years of life, Self interacts within a confined network of people and within close proximity to home. As the years pass, Self moves out into a wider social network and relates in gradually more complex situations and relationships.

Immediate Environments

The immediate environments of the MK developmental ecology include the home and nuclear family relationships, as well as the mission agency network and friendships with host country nationals who live or work close to the home. In the concentric circle model this dimension of the developmental ecology is represented by circle "B".

MKs who are brought to a host country at some point during childhood are thrown immediately into this dimension of the MK ecology. MKs who are born to missionaries already living in a host country will move into this dimension gradually. Initially the MK will just connect with the nuclear family but gradually he or she will develop relationships with other people of significance.

The teacher – MK dyad…Rosalea reflecting as an adult

Teachers can be strict without being unkind, I discovered during my year in 6th grade. Up until I was in 3rd grade I'd done my school work around the kitchen table with my mother supervising, except for the time I'd spent at a school in Australia. Grade three was my first year at an international school, a school established to offer curriculum of an internationally recognized standard. During grade three my class had a string of teachers, none of whom stayed more than a few weeks or months. Did I learn anything that year? I never have been sure. One of those teachers didn't even speak English. She was a kind, older Swedish lady who seemed as frustrated by the inability to communicate as we were. I presume her primary role was to ensure our safety because we didn't do much academic work while she was with us.

Mrs. McGregor was to be my 4th grade teacher and I enjoyed a few months with her. She was a gentle-spirited woman with a head full of long, silky, red hair. She took me aside one day and told me she was sorry I was going back to Australia for my parents' leave before we could finish a full year together. She said she'd looked forward to teaching me as a means of repaying my mother's kindness to her a number of years earlier. She had become a new mother while living in a remote location of Papua New Guinea, very close to where my family had lived. Her husband had been one of the Australian government representatives in the area. My mother had been kind to her as she had gradually gained confidence as a new mother, living in such remoteness, far from her own extended family.

But it was my 6th grade teacher who first taught me the potential of strength within a relationship between teacher and child. We never needed to guess where her boundaries lay. She had high standards for us in every area of our lives. There were no excuses accepted for laziness or forgetfulness, school work was set to be completed and to be completed to the best of our ability. She knew we each had different academic and social capacity and she catered to these but she never accepted less than the standard at which we were individually capable of achieving. Some days she frightened me but most days she motivated me. She taught us utmost respect, for authority, and for each other. No unkindness was tolerated. One had to grow while under her tutelage. Her strictness was second to none, her kindness was offered discreetly but unequivocally.

We were a room full of strong young people. More than half of us came from the homes of missionary families and we already had firm personal commitments to God and the Christian faith. Some were more radical than others, wanting to force their beliefs on our classmates. It was a point of tension between us as we debated the relative merits of sharing our Christian faith with militant force or offering gentle persuasion. The aggression between the two camps only served to destroy what efforts any of us made to guide others toward the Christian faith. She left enough time and space for the debate to expand and then she intervened. She helped us form an entry point within the school for interested students to explore Christian teaching. She rallied the headstrong and assigned them tasks where their enthusiastic energy could be productively channeled. She took the gentler ones aside and helped them to understand the perspective of the headstrong and she restored the mutual respect that had begun to be lost. She was first our teacher and then she was our spiritual guide. Her love of God coupled with her passion for our individual development motivated her to sacrifice her lunch hours.

Who are you? And who do you want to become? She challenged me. The echo still challenges me!

Figure 6.2 The concentric circle representation of a child's developmental ecology. The immediate environment is represented as the second circle "B".

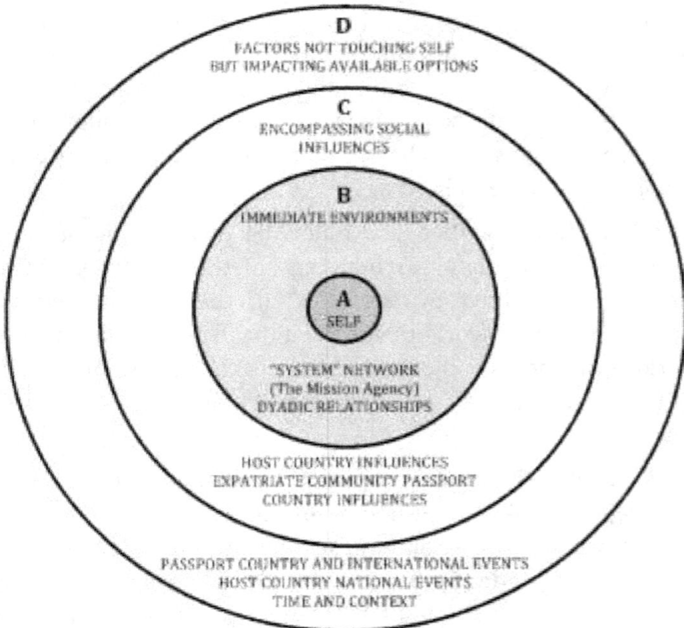

A developmental ecology incorporates relationships between the child and people of significance. In the immediate surroundings represented by "B" in Figure 6.2 the MK forms dyadic relationships.[2] A dyad is a close relationship between two individuals involving regular contact and communication.

A child has a dyadic relationship with a parent, a dyadic relationship with a sibling, a dyadic relationship with a best friend. Some dyadic relationships are stronger than others, influencing a child's development more intensely than other dyadic relationships.

> A dyad is a close relationship between two individuals involving regular contact and communication.

A primary dyad is a relationship of considerable influence. The two members of a primary dyad shape each other because they are consistently in one another's thoughts when they are in the same location and when they are absent from one another. Primary dyads steer the course of a child's development. The developing child will acquire skills, knowledge, and values from individuals with whom primary dyadic relationships have been formed. The child is motivated by these relationships. They are a powerful dynamic force in the MK developmental ecology.

Adult MKs identified the following dyadic relationships within the immediate surroundings of their developmental ecology represented by circle "B" in the model: parents, siblings, domestic workers, host country friends (parents' co-workers and neighborhood families), teachers, mission agency families, other expatriate families, and classmates (including boarding house friends).[3]

With reference to the concentric circle model (Figures 6.1 and 6.2), adult MKs identified other relationships of influence in the more remote surroundings of the developmental ecology (circle "C'): extended family members in the passport country, siblings who have already left the host country, and mission agency directors in the passport country. In the first list there is a strong connection because of a shared location and the consistent interaction that affords. In the second list there is a strong connection because of familial bonding and because of a shared life commitment.

The MK initially develops dyadic relationships with parents and siblings. In most situations these primary dyads are healthy and enduring. Most missionary parents provide loving nurture to their children and their children respond with healthy development. Most of these dyads are characterized by ongoing communication and contact throughout childhood. Such a primary dyad can be represented by overlapping circles.

Figure 6.3 Enduring dyads with ongoing influence and ongoing communication.

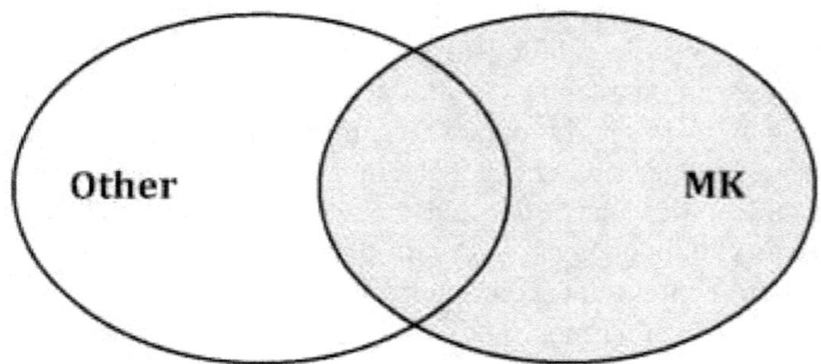

The sad reality is that some nuclear family relationships are dysfunctional and these primary dyads can be more destructive during childhood than constructive. Although the screening process mission agencies apply to missionary candidates is rigorous, it is not always comprehensive enough to sift out those who will not be nurturing parents even in their home culture, let alone in the extremes of missionary life. Consequently, there are some "Parent/MK" primary dyads that cannot be classified as enduring.

The "Sibling/MK" primary dyad is another one that is usually characterized by consistent contact and communication throughout childhood. In many cases siblings can be strong allies and comrades within the MK ecology. Their parents are doing their best to nurture and care for the development of the children but it is the children who understand each other best. The MK ecology has unique challenges and unique opportunities for enrichment. Parents observe these things through the filter of their own childhood experience and try to analyze how the children may respond and what they may need to navigate their way through their developmental years. Even in the case where an MK has one or more parents who were themselves MKs, siblings still provide the strongest empathy and understanding. Siblings are experiencing the ecology firsthand, together.

> ### Siblings are experiencing the ecology firsthand, together.

There are cases where MKs who are siblings do not form enduring dyadic relationships. The age difference between siblings can be a factor of influence. When an older sibling is living in the passport country to continue his or her education then a younger sibling can feel like this individual is no closer to him or her than extended family members. If they have shared childhood years in the host country then there may be ongoing contact and communication when the older sibling leaves but sometimes this is only through the parents who conscientiously maintain contact with the older child. The younger child may feel estranged from the older sibling. If a family moves abroad when an older sibling is at a crucial stage in education and the choice is made to leave the older sibling in the passport country, then the childhood experiences of the MK ecology are not shared. The result in this instance can also be an estrangement between siblings.

Primary dyads can also be formed between the MK and domestic workers while living in the host country. In many cases a domestic worker is employed to help with household maintenance and so the MK will have regular interaction with this adult who comes into the home and participates in the routine of family life. Typically, the domestic worker will be benevolent, even kind to the point of self-sacrifice with the MK. In some cases, the MK is left for extended periods in the sole care of the domestic worker. For example, if both missionary parents are working outside the home and the child comes home from school early in the afternoon, then the domestic worker may be required to not only provide physical care for the child, but supervision that also incorporates discipline. The

MK will have extended interaction with this adult and learn from his or her values and skills.

An adult's choice to care... Joy reflecting as a missionary mother

During our second four-year term as missionaries in Papua New Guinea, our youngest son was born. When Jeff was only a few weeks old, we were assigned to serve as hostel parents to elementary school age missionary children whose parents lived and ministered in rural areas. Knowing my limitations as "super-woman," I hired a helper named Hongoi to do general housework for our extended family. In addition to washing multiple loads of clothes per day, scrubbing wood floors, and wiping dishes, he loved to play with our plump but rather unresponsive baby boy, Jeff. Once in a while I would hear them giggling together. It was music to my ears. My mother heart wanted to disbelieve growing concerns about Jeff's development. He simply was not displaying the same eagerness to learn that had characterized our first two children; in fact, I wondered if he might be deaf due to his often-delayed reactions to simple stimulus.

Hongoi's work habits were first rate, but somehow he still managed to find time to enjoy the baby while the older children were at school. Jeff and Hongoi developed a unique relationship that centered around discovering the simple joys of life. When Jeff decided that silverware stored on the bottom cupboard shelf made a fascinating toy, Hongoi not only joined in the fun, he joyfully re-washed the stuff after their "game" ended. At 18 months of age, Jeff was diagnosed as mentally handicapped. The doctors in Australia gave us tips on how to help him learn to walk. Hongoi, our most enthusiastic volunteer in programming Jeff's motor skills each day, assisted him in putting one foot in front of the other as he held onto custom-made handrails for support. Jeff got the hang of it in a hurry and no one was more thrilled than Hongoi.

When Jeff was nearly three years old and still unable to form simple words, we returned to the States. Hongoi remained an employee of the hostel for several years before he decided to go to Bible School and become a

pastor. Jeff received special education and graduated from high school. Years later, we returned to Papua New Guinea to visit. Jeff joined us for that trip. The first person to greet us when we stepped off the plane was Hongoi. The delight on both of their faces was beyond description. Jeff didn't want to let Hongoi out of his sight.

As I reflect, I am aware that the one-on-one attention that Jeff needed for optimum mental and physical development had been provided in a very personal way by our domestic helper – long before we were even aware he needed it. And we, Jeff's parents, will always be grateful.

The dyadic relationship with domestic workers is seldom enduring. It seldom involves ongoing influence and communication. For a season of the MK's life there has been a primary dyadic relationship with this adult, they have remained in each other's thoughts and the relationship has influenced the child's development. However, at some point in life the domestic worker has moved on to another job, returned to a home area, or taken up greater responsibilities in his or her own home. Alternatively, the missionary family may leave the area, or decide the domestic worker is no longer necessary in the family routine. Whatever the circumstances, the dyad of MK/domestic worker, in most cases, eventually comes to an end. In adult life it is often impossible for the MK to even find the domestic worker again much less reconnect with him or her. The dyad has been broken, and is therefore classified as temporal.

Temporal dyads can be represented with a jagged line between the two participants.

Figure 6.4 Temporal dyads with influence through a period of contact and resultant memories, but time constrained interaction and limited or no ongoing communication.

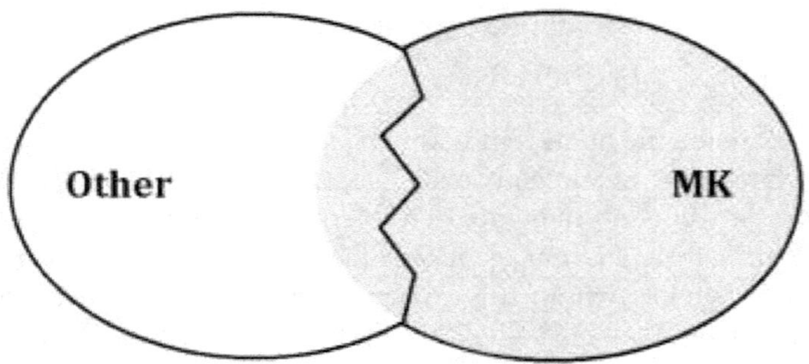

It is important to draw the distinction between enduring and temporal dyads. It is within dyadic relationships that the MK learns lifelong patterns of social interaction and emotional attachment. Within the home, the immediate surroundings, the MK learns the most enduring lessons about relationships. This can probably be said of all children. The MK learns that primary dyadic relationships can be formed with people who are related and some who are not. Sometimes stronger dyads are formed with non-family members. Dyadic relationships can be powerful for a season of life and then fall into estrangement.

Within enduring dyads, the MK has the opportunity to learn skills that facilitate life-long relationships. Within these dyads there can be reciprocal care and mutual trust. There is the chance to learn social skills that assist in conflict resolution, heightened communication capacity, and the art of compromise for the sake of partnership. However, if these enduring dyadic relationships are only between the MK as a child and an adult, such as a parent, then there is always the disadvantage of age discrepancy and the power that factor naturally ascribes to the adult in the dyad. This is one of the key factors in understanding how the MK ecology leads to the adult outcomes described earlier in the book. It is in the life patterns of childhood that adult character traits begin to take shape. For well-rounded development the MK needs to have healthy, enduring dyadic relationships with those who are age equivalent as well as with significant adults.

It is in the life patterns of
childhood that adult character
traits begin to take shape.

Outside the home, but within close proximity to the home, MKs have the opportunity to develop dyadic relationships with a variety of other individuals: host country friends, adults and children from mission agency families, teachers, children from other families within the expatriate community, and school classmates. In almost all of these instances the dyads could be classified as temporal dyads. In almost all these instances, the relationship is strong, with regular interaction, and of powerful influence, for a season of the MK's life. Then it ends, sometimes abruptly. For a season the MK has been motivated by a particular relationship, learned skills, acquired knowledge, and absorbed values from an individual. In the case of a dyadic relationship with another child there has been a season during which there has been reciprocal involvement in each other's development. Then, one or the other, or both move on and the MK must establish other dyads.

MKs from different families who have shared a location during childhood years try desperately to keep in touch if there has been an attachment formed. In some cases, this is possible and both MKs are richer for the enduring dyad. However, even if there is a reconnection established later in life, there is often a gap in communication and interaction, so the dyad is classified as temporal.

It is the general experience of MKs that there are more temporal dyads throughout developmental years than there are enduring ones. In these experiences, the MK learns what he or she believes to be true about relationships. Dyadic relationships can be linked to the outcomes of the MK ecology as listed in Table 3.1.

Within the dyadic relationships of the MK ecology, the child learns that people of all races are to be valued and there can be intimate connection no matter what nationality the two people within a dyad come from. Though children may learn this in a mono-cultural setting it is not so deeply embedded in the psyche as in the MK experience. The childhood ecology therefore, is linked to the adult outcomes of tolerance and acceptance of difference, cross-cultural skills, a value of multiculturalism, and an inclusive relational capacity. Within the dyadic relationships of childhood, the MK establishes a worldwide network of friends, learns to adapt to the needs of the moment, and learns to make the most of immediate situations because one never knows how long a friendship or particular context will last.

The MK may experience few enduring dyads but these relationships are often of heightened significance because there are so few consistent people in the child's life. Within these relationships there is the potential for a deep level of trust between the two individuals. There is the opportunity for the other member of the dyad to help the MK grow in self-awareness. Both adults and other children can help the MK to reach his or her potential as an individual, within enduring dyads. These dyadic relationships also hold the potential for strong Christian discipleship. The early and deep awareness of spirituality that accompanies the MK childhood can be harnessed and built into a strong, healthy, Christian faith if the MK is encouraged to process the God-factor within enduring dyads. Trust and mutual acceptance are the defining elements of these relationships. They are a powerful force.

> Trust and mutual acceptance
> are the defining elements of
> these relationships.

*An adult's choice to befriend...*Rosalea as a teenager

I'd cleaned the room and made up a bed for her but she didn't want to stay in the guest room. She wanted to sleep in the spare bed I kept in my room. She laughed as she asked me to make up the spare bed in my room. We were friends. She'd earned the right to ask for whatever she wanted.

We lay in our beds that night exchanging stories and seeking one another's opinion on the events and people that made up our shared world. She'd been a witness to the 17 years of my life, from birth. She'd encouraged and chastened along the way, celebrating milestones and sharing the burden of hurts. She was my friend. She was important to me, as I was to her. She laughed as she told me again that my older sister was still her favorite. I laughed too. I knew that was true and I was glad it was true. We both missed my sister who had moved to Australia three years earlier.

We laughed together as we remembered the times my sister and I had ridden as pillion passengers on the motorbike my father used to navigate along the rough roads in the Fugwa valley, when we were small. The other adult missionaries each had their own motorbikes and we'd travel in convoy sometimes. There was the time my father was asked about the number of wives he had when he'd driven the tractor out to the Australian government station with my mother, the single missionary women, and my siblings and me in a trailer attached to the back of the tractor. She'd shared so many Christmases and birthdays in our home. She'd eaten the not-quite-right baked goods my sister and I had prepared in the cast iron stoves that had to be kept heated at just-the-right temperature by feeding just-the-right amount of wood into it throughout the baking process. She'd asked me about the choices I made during my teenage years but never judged.

Now she was leaving. She was on her way back to Australia, to live, after many years of working in Papua New Guinea. I would leave in a year myself but I didn't expect her to be gone before me. It was not how either of us had expected it. The timing had not been her choice and I was sure there was pain. Where was she going to live? What would she be doing for work? Was she okay about all of this? I shaped the questions and anticipated the expressions of pain, but they were never voiced, not even a hint.

She told me of her deep love of God and her trust that He works through people to achieve His purpose on this earth. She read from her Bible and her devotional book to show me how God had spoken to her and reassured her of His sovereignty. She'd chosen not to harbor the pain or to allow the hurt to manifest in ungraciousness. I lay quietly, thinking about how her love of God was, once again, an amazing example to me. She'd been a witness to my life, but I had been a witness to hers as well. She'd made choices, throughout my 17 years, to model godliness to me.

I thought about the Bible and devotional book that rested on the shelf just beside my head. She'd played a significant role in teaching me the value of learning, daily, from my Bible. Even as she prepared to leave PNG, amidst a time that was confusing to both of us, she showed me that she was my friend, and she showed me that a deep trust in God was of more value than anything else in life.

We would never have had that conversation, except that she chose to stay in my room. We would never have had that conversation, except that she chose, 17 years ago, to be my friend.

Temporal dyads also leave an imprint on the adult MK profile. Temporal dyads are not necessarily unhealthy or destructive. All dyads are relationships of significance. The challenge arises for the MK when there is an extended period of life characterized by temporal dyads, significant relationships that are shared for a season and then ended. Other children may experience a similar pattern of relational initiation and ending in their childhood and the outcome may be similar. It is merely listed here as a defining element of the MK culture and not necessarily unique to it.

As a result of serial temporal dyadic relationships, the MK can assume a diminished sense of belonging in any one place and amongst any one group of people. Each of these people has been significant for a season and has reciprocated the need for the relationship. Within these dyads the seeds of ongoing mobility are planted within the MK. Friendships and locations are not continuous. The MK learns that a high turnover of friendships is an acceptable pattern. The long-term consequence of this is that the MK can learn to just move on rather than resolve conflict within relationships. The MK can learn that it is painful to become too closely attached to people and things of significance because there is not likely to be any lasting relationship or ongoing contact. The realization of this may not be overt but rather, is likely to be a subliminal message that runs through the MK's psyche.

Temporal dyads can be accompanied by a great deal of pain during the childhood experiences of the MK. Friends come and go. Teachers come and go. Pets come and go. Locations of importance come and go. The separations and endings are seldom properly grieved. The common belief is that children are adaptable and they will bounce back after the unavoidable period of pain. The common belief is that children really only need their immediate family for a sense of social security.

It is from these experiences MKs carry into adulthood unresolved grief and patterns of dealing with pain that may handicap adult relationships. The MK has learned that close relationships that are valued hold the potential for the most intense pain. They have a heightened anticipation that relationships will end and sometimes abruptly. In adult relationships MKs apply the relational self-protection that they have learned as survival skills during childhood. They exercise independence to the point of self-sufficiency, pushing aside those who want to share mutual support within adult dyadic relationships. They apply learned behavior that protects them against relational vulnerability. They must be in control of their own world. Only by this means can they manage the inevitable pain of separation.

Dyadic relationships both enrich and challenge the developmental ecology of the MK childhood. They lead to significant adult outcomes because of the powerful force they exert on child development. The following chapter moves on to explore the life of the MK in the wider networks within which he or she moves as social independence emerges.

> Dyadic relationships both enrich
> and challenge the developmental
> ecology of the MK childhood.

Chapter 7: **More remote factors within the MK ecology**

Encompassing Social Influences

As a child matures he or she will move further from the home to fulfill social needs. Over time the child adds to his or her social network and begins to engage in gradually more complex relationships.[1] The young child interacts with a few friends chosen by his or her parents but as time passes the child begins to choose his or her own friends and also begins to engage in friendship groups. This gradual progression into more and more complex relational patterns is part of the socialization process that all children engage in as they mature. For the MK the path towards social maturity can be both enriched and constrained.

> For the MK the path towards
> social maturity can be both
> enriched and constrained.

In Figure 7.1 the emergence into a broader social network is represented by circle "C". The MK has a growing awareness and assertion of self (A) within the childhood ecology and deepening dyadic relationships with those who share the home environment (B). Gradually there is opportunity to interact more independently in settings outside the home. For the MK this introduces opportunities to mix with teachers, school peers, coaches and fellow participants in sport and cultural interests.

Figure 7.1 The concentric circle representation of a child's developmental ecology. The encompassing social influences are represented as the third circle "C".

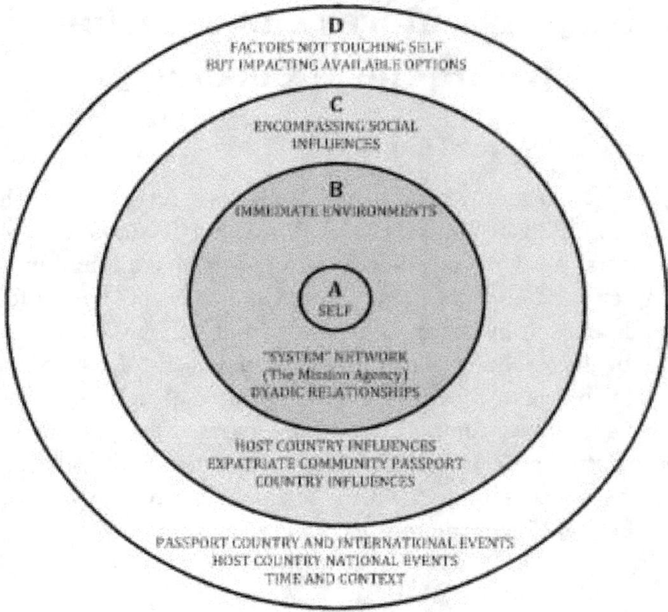

Each of the relationships represented in circle "C" is set within a specific location-related context and the MK begins to absorb and manifest appropriate social protocol for each location. This can include social protocol appropriate to school, church, home, the homes of other expatriate friends, and the homes of host country national friends or parents' work associates. The MK also has to learn to negotiate the social demands of the broader contexts represented by a passport country and a host country. Often the expectations in each setting are quite different and require considerable adjustment in social behavior as the child moves between the two contexts.

In the passport country the MK is usually engaged in social relationships with extended family members. These are relationships of significance even although there may be inconsistent communication between the MK and extended family members throughout the MK's childhood. There is at the very least a biological connection. Sometimes these relationships are deep and meaningful such that the MK is significantly impacted by the relationship during developmental years. Some extended family members visit the area where the MK lives in the host country and therefore have firsthand knowledge of the MK's life. Some extended family members and MKs make considerable effort to maintain communication once they are separated. However, often the distance and vastly different life experiences between the MK and biological relatives make it challenging to form close bonds. The MK is faced with the opportunity to learn to negotiate social interaction with extended family members even when there may be little depth of insight into one another's worldview. This impacts the MK's social development and shapes adult perceptions about expectations within relationships.

The mission agency network to which the MK belongs in the host country extends to a network of people in the passport country. The MK has opportunity to engage socially with personnel who work in the mission agency offices within the passport country. The MK may not see these individuals any more frequently than extended family members. In these relationships the connection is not biological, but rather it is the mission priority. The MK may feel a sense of belonging within the framework of the mission even when in the passport country if there is opportunity to interact with staff from the mission agency and with other missionaries who are in the passport country at the same time.

A similar social connection may develop with particular church people who strongly support the work of the missionary family. Some pastoral and lay people within the passport country follow the work of particular missionary families closely and can engage in informed interaction with members of the missionary family when they are together. Sometimes this connection is only through the MK's parents but sometimes there is a significant connection with the MK himself or herself.

Unusual social connections... Rosalea reflecting as an adult

She had read every one of my letters included with my parents' quarterly newsletter to their supporters throughout my childhood years. She could name my pet dog, my friends, and my favorite play activities. She knew where I had been to school and where each of my siblings had moved to in order to finish their education. She had followed my family throughout my parents' missionary career. And she had prayed for us, prayed for each member of the family. I was overwhelmed by the thought of someone, who was a stranger to me, having been an informed prayer intercessor for such a sustained period of time. And now she wanted to continue her powerful ministry for my husband and sons, and for me.

I was too humbled to try to explain how much her commitment meant to me and so I recounted for her some of the challenge my mother had faced to get those paragraphs out of each of her children for inclusion in her quarterly newsletters. It was always holiday time. The family was together after months of separation with one or all of us away at school. We played games, we roamed the mission compound, and we joined ball games on the hardpacked dirt surface of the playing field. There was no time to sit at a table and press our pens hard into the stencil so that she could immortalize our musings on the mimeograph and produce hundreds of pages to post to people we didn't know. And even if we found time to pull together some descriptions of our daily routine that could be of interest to no one, we would then have to sit around the table for hours licking the envelopes and applying the postage stamps. Addresses had to be individually written and return addresses had to be stamped on the envelopes.

The only highlight in the process was watching the big canvas bag bulge as we loaded the finished product into it so that the mailman could hoist the bag over his shoulder and carry it off down the road when he made his weekly hike to the post office at the government post. The bag was packed in the evening and he would arrive early the next day to begin the hike to the government post. Late in the afternoon, as the clouds began to roll in, he'd hike back up the slight incline to our home to bring whatever he'd collected at the post office. We'd dump the contents on the floor while our mother paid the mailman for his efforts. The mail was sorted into piles, one for each family who lived on the mission compound, and we'd each be allocated a family to whom to deliver mail. Sometimes we'd scamper off together and deliver one and then another's. We were always welcomed into a home on mail day. But we didn't linger, because night falls quickly when you live amidst the mountain ranges.

The mission compound's diesel driven generator would be cranked into life around 6 pm and a light bulb would illuminate the kitchen just when it was getting too dark to see if the vegetables were boiling on the big cast iron stove. We'd help to stoke the fire with additional pieces of chopped wood and we'd make sure there was water on to boil to do the washing up afterwards. The copper pot would simmer away at the edge of the stove, full of water that we would use for our evening ablutions.

Preparing a shower was a process. You had to carry your portion of hot water to the bathroom and pour it into the aluminum bucket then add some cold water to get just the right temperature for bathing. You had to hoist the full bucket up to just the right height and then secure the rope around a hook fixed to the frame of the shower recess. Once under the shower you would reach up and spin the shower rose that had been especially fitted to the bottom of the bucket to allow the water to trickle down. You learned early that it was best to release just enough water to moisten your skin and then close the shower rose while you lathered and scrubbed. Then you could release the rest of the water to rinse clean. Rain water was collected in a corrugated tank outside the house and during the wet season it was always full to capacity but during the rest of the year water had to be conserved to meet all the needs of the home.

Our home life during the holiday times was a pleasant routine to us. However, it provided some amusement when we had overseas guests come to stay who didn't understand the intricacies of managing our environment. There was the six-foot-two-inch tall evangelist who complained to us that it was hard to wash the top half of his body under the shower. We'd carried his water and helped him fill the bucket to the right temperature and then politely left him to the privacy of the bathroom. No one had thought to tell him that the bucket needed to be hoisted and secured above head height before opening the shower rose to release the water.

There was the kind, elderly visiting pastor's wife who appeared on Sunday morning dressed for church. I whispered to my mother that she should offer the lady a pair of my shoes to wear because she would surely hurt her ankles navigating the storm engraved roads of the local area in her high heels. She hadn't known the conditions and we wanted to protect her.

Others came who should have been more aware and we were less generous with these ones. There was the visiting preacher who presented the "12 steps to a holy life." When you sit through a sermon that is translated into three languages and you understand all of them, the 12 steps become 36 steps as translation necessitates adjustments in wording, and you care very little about living a holy life after the first hour of the sermon and much less by the time you are finally able to get home and light the fire in the cast iron stove to begin cooking Sunday lunch fit for guests.

That type of guest was rare. For the most part our holiday life was full of memorable days and evenings. The missionary families loved to gather for games together, or singing. Singing in your own language becomes something you treasure when worship is usually in an adopted style and tongue. My mother had a little pump organ that we would unfold from the suitcase size wooden box, into a freestanding organ that had to be peddled much like a treadle sewing machine in order to generate volume as the keys were pressed. Some truly accomplished pianists were able to modify their generous styles to play the old hymns on that limited keyboard. Watching the faces of those missionaries taught me a love of the old hymns and a value of one's personal heritage. No one resented the foreign worship styles but they all absorbed the pleasure of the familiar. I learned that you can have a different kind of love for people and practices and none has to be valued more highly than another. The missionary families were our comrades and our extended family. The people we lived amongst, those we served, were equally valued.

Holiday time always came to an end and the last few days were devoted to haircuts, checking the wardrobe to see what was too short or what needed mending. New clothes had to have name tags sewed on as did our blankets. Bags had to be packed and decisions made as to what stayed in this home and what came to the home in town where we would live for the next ten weeks or so.

These were the routines of life that were so familiar and yet it never crossed our minds to describe any of this in our newsletter paragraphs. We didn't think any of it newsworthy, so we described the antics of our pet dog and cat who grew up together and intimidated each other. To us, our life was just average, a routine we managed, with people we enjoyed and valued.

In some cases, the communication with church families can be only one way. However, there are instances where the communication is two ways. The MK may develop a bond with a particular church family over the years and the social exchanges can be significant in the development of this child. Such interactions add to the richness and the complexity of social networks that foster social maturity within the MK.

Enriched but complex connections... Ruth reflecting as an adult

We had a tin box which contained a card file for our "Prayer Partners." This card file was divided into sections for my mother and father and a section for each of us children. The cards had the names and addresses of people in other countries, mainly USA, who had picked us to write to and pray for and sometimes send gift boxes. I loved to look through that file and read the names and addresses and imagine what the people were like and wonder if I would ever meet them.

I had two Prayer Partners who were special, Pam and Phyllis. They were special because they were consistent with their letters and gift boxes for many years through my growing up years in Papua New Guinea. Other Prayer Partners wrote once or twice and then I never heard from

them again. I wrote to Pam till we were about 16 and then slowly our letters stopped.

Phyllis was extra special because not only was she my Prayer Partner but her younger sister was my younger sister's Prayer Partner and her mother was my mother's Prayer Partner. The year I turned 17, my mother handed me an envelope which she had received from Phyllis' mother and in it was a letter to me.

Phyllis' mother was writing to tell me that Phyllis had been killed in a fatal car accident where a drunken driver had run through a red light. She described how Phyllis had just been accepted into the Marines and was enjoying her life and looking forward to what her opportunities would be. She described the funeral service and the Christian witness it had been to many of Phyllis' friends. I remember wishing I could have been there to say goodbye. I really felt the loss of this friend whom I had never met but knew well, one with whom I had a close connection. Even now as I write this I have tears in my eyes as I remember that loss. Even though we never met face to face, Phyllis was special to me.

While in the host country the MK develops social connections with a variety of people outside the home environment. Once the child starts school, teachers begin to contribute to the social development of the MK. In some settings teachers are seen inside and outside of the school setting. They are part of the expatriate community and therefore mix socially with the MK and his or her family. In some instances, schools are set up to cater for the needs of groups of MKs and expatriate children within a given location. Teachers are specially recruited for these settings. In the case of MK schools, teachers will come to the location because of a calling or passion for the mission work. In these instances, teachers have an intentional and significant impact on the development of the child. Teachers will take an active interest in the holistic development of the child. Teachers spend many hours a week with the child and the potential to impact is heightened because of the significance of time together.

> In these instances, teachers have an
> intentional and significant impact on
> the development of the child.

Other adults become engaged in the development of the MK within the host country. As the MK grows older he or she develops special interests such as in sports, music, art, or any number of possible hobbies. The MK may engage in social interaction with a teacher of cultural skills, or a coach, or a friendly adult who has a particular skill and is willing to pass on insights to the child. Sometimes these are expatriates and sometimes these are host country nationals. The MK has regular interaction with such adults and is shaped by the social exchanges.

Age equivalent peers significantly shape the development of the MK and these relationships also fall within circle "C" in Figure 7.1. Friendships are formed with those who are most accessible to the child. These can be within the local church or ministry setting within which the missionary family is engaged, the mission agency network, within the school environment, or within other social settings where the MK or missionary family is engaged. The MK may have friends from many different nationalities or walks of life. As with any child, the MK will have a few close friends and then a broader social group within which he or she interacts. There is a close attachment formed with a few friends and then a social role to play within a wider network of friendships.

Within peer attachment and continuity in social networks children learn and reinforce the behavior patterns and identity of one another.[2] The social demands from friends exert considerable demand on the child. There is a hierarchy of influence exerted over the developing child from best friend through to the widest social network. This is a significant concept to understand in the case of the MK because the best friend can come from a significantly different home environment than the MK and may represent significantly different social and spiritual values. In a mono-cultural context it is more likely that a child will be drawn to a best friend who represents similar social and spiritual values. This is, of course, not always the case. However, for the MK close peer attachment represents an area of potential vulnerability.

> There is a hierarchy of influence
> exerted over the developing child
> from best friend through to the
> widest social network.

In the MK context peer attachment can be formed with host country nationals. Small children love to play with one another and they are less aware of cultural, social, and economic differences than are adults. When an MK forms a close attachment with a host country national, at some point as they grow older, there will be tensions to resolve within the relationship that relate to the disparities in their cultural, social, and economic status. This is not insurmountable but adds an element of vulnerability to the process of social maturity for the MK.

MKs often form close peer attachments to other MKs. The family values and socio-economic status within mission networks are usually closely aligned so there is little or no tension to resolve in these areas. When two MKs become best-friends there is considerable influence exerted over each other's social and spiritual development. They challenge one another's emerging worldview and hold one another accountable spiritually. They understand each other's joy and pain because they are living the experience together. Theirs is a shared history.

In both of the abovementioned contexts, the MK then belongs to a wider network or friendship group and there is a social hierarchy that influences the development of the child. The child finds his or her position within this hierarchy and functions according to related social demands from his or her peers. This however, introduces a further area of vulnerability for the MK. It is in the continuity in friendship groups that behavior patterns and identity are reinforced. When friendship networks are dissolved, the developing child is significantly impacted. This happens repeatedly in the experience of the MK.

The high turnover of friends because of the excessive mobility of expatriate families means that the social networks within which the MK is engaged are regularly being dissolved and new ones constructed. The child consistently has to find his or her place within the social strata. The reinforcement of social behavior and identity affirmation that peers provide for one another happens erratically throughout the MK childhood rather than in a fluid pattern.

> It is in the continuity in friendship
> groups that behavior patterns and
> identity are reinforced.

Attachment to non-familial adults is another area of social development in which the MK is greatly impacted. In the mono-cultural setting a non-familial adult may take a special interest in a child and the child's self-esteem can be strengthened because this relationship is chosen rather than biologically ascribed as is the case in relationships with adults who are related. In the MK context there is heightened opportunity for such chosen relationships because of the absence of extended family. Most missionary and other expatriate families miss their extended family and so intentionally seek contact with others who can become surrogate family. Adult expatriates will often form attachments with particular MKs and provide input into their social development. Adults who are host country nationals can also form close attachments with MKs. When an MK is aware that he or she has been specifically chosen for such a relationship then behaviors that support the relationship are reinforced, identity is affirmed, and self-worth is enhanced. These attachments exert a powerful influence on the MK's path toward social maturity.

Attachments with adults, familial and non-familial, provide the child with opportunity to experience a gradual shift in power that ultimately leads to social autonomy. Over time the child grows in confidence within the social exchanges shared with an adult and gradually begins to experiment with personal assertion. Influential adults guide the child in choosing appropriate behavior and establish healthy boundaries for social exchange. As the child engages in progressively more complex interactions with influential adults, social identity is formed. Over time within healthy attachments, there is a gradual shift in power within the relational behavior of the child and the adult. The two become friends rather than influential adult and emerging individual. Gradually the child learns to engage as a socially mature individual within the relationship.

> As the child engages in progressively more
> complex interactions with influential
> adults, social identity is formed.

Once again, the issue of mobility impacts the power of attachments in the social development of the child. Adults come and go in and out of the life of the MK throughout childhood. Expatriate families are on different contractual cycles and so the MK cannot guarantee being consistently engaged socially with the same adults over an enduring period of time. The MK comes and goes from the passport country as the missionary family completes terms of contract within the host country. Sometimes the family returns to the same location in the host country and sometimes it does not. Even in the case of social attachment with host country adults, there is an erratic pattern to the emerging maturity of the MK, within the relationship. Opportunities to develop close attachments that facilitate gradual shifts in social power over the passage of time are limited. The path toward social maturity is enriched by the potential breadth of adults and peers with whom to form attachments but challenged by the obstacles to continuous social engagement.

Figure 7.2 The concentric circle representation of a child's developmental ecology. The broadest influences of time and context are represented as the outer circle "D".

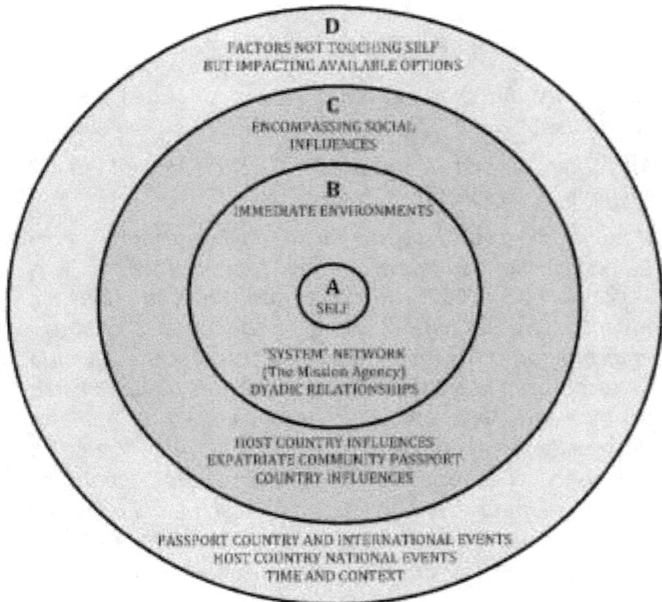

Available Options

Every life is lived within an historical time and context. The outer circle of the concentric circle model "D" (Figure 7.2) represents significant factors of time and context within which the MK life is lived. The backdrop of the MK life includes the social and political climate of both the passport and the host country and how these influence life choices for the MK. "D" also includes any historical events that occur throughout the MK's developmental years that impact available options. It represents the timing of significant personal and family events in the life of the MK and the accumulation of events over time that impact MK development. It represents the God-factor that is the reason for the MK existence. "D" is the backdrop to the MK life.

Notable events happen around the globe on a daily basis. Some of these events have long term consequences on countries and people but some of them merely punctuate the passing of time.

Time and place... Rosalea as a child

"Dad, why did that policeman stand to attention and salute us?"

My father turned to acknowledge the question but did not respond as he continued driving.

We had borrowed a car for a day's outing in Port Moresby, the capital of Papua New Guinea. It was September 15th, 1975, the day before PNG was to become independent, a self-governing nation. As a country emerging onto the international political scene it would be recognized as a Commonwealth nation, having been a protectorate of Australia. It was to become an independently recognized country with British allegiance. The Queen of England would remain as sovereign figurehead. PNG and Australia had been preparing and planning for this occasion for some time and the celebrations in the capital city took center stage. By chance, my family was in Port Moresby for this significant event, en-route to Australia for my parents' four yearly leave.

"Dad, all the policemen are standing to attention and saluting us as we drive past."

Policemen formed an official guard along the road leading to the Parliament House. PNG was showcasing their first national Parliament building for their independence celebrations. The celebrations also included presentations of tribal dancing in the Sir Hubert Murray Stadium. There was to be a lowering of the Australian flag on the night of the 15th and PNG's own red, black, and yellow flag, displaying the bird of paradise and the stars of the Southern Cross, would be raised on the 16th. At the international school we'd been proudly singing "This is our flag, flag of our land..." for some months. As we'd driven about all morning, people milling around the city had been smiling and waving plastic miniatures of the PNG flag.

"Dad, the car behind us has an Australian flag attached to it and the one following that has a flag with only the Union Jack on it."

Suddenly my father realized where we were. He'd inadvertently entered a road immediately ahead of the convoy of cars leading Prince Charles to the new Parliament House. Prince Charles was representing his mother, Queen Elizabeth II, on this official occasion. The police were snapping to attention to salute the royal representative. The car with the very unofficial missionary family was leading the convoy toward the new Parliament House for its inspection by the royal dignitary.

There was no way to exit this major thoroughfare so we smiled and waved back to each policeman who saluted.

The next day I watched Prince Charles from afar as we sat on the grass near the Sir Hubert Murray Stadium. I wondered what he thought of the tribal dancing that was so familiar to me but must have been strange to him. I wondered if he wasn't just plain hot, standing there in the sunshine and humidity of this coastal town, watching Michael Somare sign the Declaration of Allegiance and take up office as the first Prime Minister for PNG. What was such an engulfing world for me could have been just plain boring to him. He never did smile as far as I could tell.

Later, during my teenage years, I was running to escape an unannounced thunderstorm that had interrupted a presentation by Queen Elizabeth II herself, in Mt. Hagen when I looked over to the road and met the smiling eyes of Prince Phillip. He waved and I waved back, him safe and dry in his official black car, and me, soaked to the skin running toward home.

The social and political climate of both the passport and the host country, have an indirect impact on the developmental ecology of the MK. Socio-economic conditions in the passport country account for the standard of living missionary families experience. The passport country's political influence in the international arena impacts the status that the missionary family has within the host country. Social conditions in the passport country impact the daily life of MK in terms of adjustments that need to be made in things as basic as standard of dress and eating patterns when moving between the passport and host countries. What is acceptable and valued in one country may not be in another and the MK may need to make considerable adjustment and internally reconcile why such an adjustment is necessary. The political climate of some countries is unstable; the social climate of some countries can endorse corruption; the religious climate of some countries can be intolerant. Within the global arena some countries are hostile or suspicious of one another. In each of these instances the indirect impact on the MK can be considerable.

In some instances, the life of the MK can be considerably restricted because of the factors represented in circle "D". For example, where there is serious concern for the safety of the child there will be considerable protective measures put in place. Availability of social interaction options may be restricted. The MK has no choice over this and lives within the confines of the developmental ecology. Another example may be where a male MK is living in a host culture where men are the authority figures in their families. When the father is away from the home the oldest male child then fills the role of head of the home, speaking on behalf of the family, even for his mother. Once the guests leave, the male child then has to resume the role of child under the authority of his mother. To be accepted within the culture the MK must fulfill the role of oldest male child. To retain a connection with the passport culture, and to interact fairly with his mother, he must adjust between the diverse social expectations as required. The purposefulness of the missionary life requires that MKs adjust socially according to the demands of the host country and yet have the capacity to competently negotiate the social demands of the passport country.

Historic events also impact child development and they are represented by circle "D" in the model, as a backdrop to the MK experience. World War II affected many countries and after the war mission sending agencies deployed personnel to the poorest and most affected areas. During colonial years religious bodies deployed personnel to countries that were being colonized. Natural disasters occur randomly around the world and in their wake religious agencies send families abroad to assist in humanitarian aid and spiritual care for the victims. Civil wars, moral decline, issues of discrimination, and the advancement of alternative religious beliefs all draw attention to particular countries at different times in history and subsequently affect the policies of mission sending agencies. MKs are raised within countries that have the world or the evangelical church's attention at a specific time in history. History impacts the MK ecology.

Mamba memories…Tyler reflecting as an adult

When I was two and my sister less than a year old, my parents took us to a church conference that involved camping out in a tent. This was in Zambia, during my parents' first term as missionaries. In the afternoons, while Mom attended meetings with pastors' wives or led children's services, my sister napped in a fold-up playpen in the tent. The arrangement worked well; the meetings were outside and close to the tent, so Mom could hear if Martha stirred or woke.

One afternoon, midway through the week, Mom stepped into the tent to see how her little baby was doing and found a visitor. A mamba, one of the deadliest snakes in Africa, probably attracted by my sister's warmth, had curled up next to her in the playpen. Mom immediately sounded the battle cry, "Snake! Snake!" People came running, carrying sticks and shovels, whips and rakes ready to beat the offender to death, but the sneaky mamba slipped through a hole in the tent and escaped into the grass. We never saw him again. In later years, my family told this story around the table at holidays, as a funny family memory, "remember the time when . . ." It ranked up there with the time Grandpa saw a cobra in the grass and started running from it. The faster Grandpa ran, the faster the cobra followed. His cries of "Snake! Snake!" brought the usual assortment of shovels and sticks. And after the locals dispatched the cobra, they realized the poor thing had tried to bite Grandpa in the ankle and had caught its teeth in his pant leg. It wasn't chasing him at all.

One Thanksgiving, as we were sitting around the desiccated turkey carcass telling funny family stories, we had a knock at the front door. Most people used our back door for visits and we weren't expecting anyone, so my father said to me, "Johnny, go see who that is." I opened the door to find a cobra, hood extended, striking at his reflection in the glass. Of course, I called "Snake! Snake!" with the usual results.

Surprisingly, I can't remember ever hearing of someone we knew dying from a snakebite. One of the younger missionary kids came home one day with two telltale puncture wounds on his knee, but he couldn't remember being bitten and he didn't even get a red ring around the wounds. However, living with so many close calls, certainly affected my view of the world.

Growing up in Zambia, I never believed the fantasy that the world is safe. Every time I climbed a tree or walked in the grass, I watched for the movement of death slithering by. When my friend Mark stepped on a puff adder one night as he was walking barefoot behind the schoolhouse, my response was not sympathy but chastisement for walking at night without a flashlight. At least Mark was barefoot and felt the snake underfoot in time to jump away before the sleepy adder struck. We all agreed, if he'd been wearing shoes it could have been much worse, but if he'd been carrying a flashlight it would have been much better.

Choosing to ride my bicycle to a friend's house a mile away, even though it meant peddling fast past the woods where a legendary man-killing mamba lived, prepared me for the trips to Lusaka my family would later make. On those trips, it was human man-killers lurking in the woods who frightened us as we drove fast to get to our destination safely.

In the late 1970s, the Rhodesian Civil War was more than a decade old, and guerillas had set up semi-permanent camps in the forests of southern Zambia. Fighting against white apartheid in Rhodesia, the guerillas hated white people, whether Rhodesian soldiers or American missionaries. The newspapers had already reported the rape and killing of a Baptist missionary couple captured on the country's only highway near Livingstone on the border with Rhodesia, but our mission hospital needed medicine and the only way to get it was to drive the highway to Lusaka.

We always traveled as a family in those final years of the war because of the constant warnings from the American Consulate and rumors of personnel evacuations. Once, when Martha and I were fifty miles away at school, the consulate had called and issued a travel ban; they'd received "credible threats" against Americans. My parents drove to our school in defiance of the ban and stayed with us until the warning was lifted. After that, we traveled together whenever possible, particularly if Dad had to go to Lusaka, which was a good eight hours from our house.

Most of the route was relatively safe, since we were driving away from Livingstone, and we figured we'd drive fast through the one stretch of road where the guerillas lived (like riding fast past the mamba's lair). We also left early enough to be safely in Lusaka long before sunset.

Unfortunately, as we climbed the hills up into the guerilla forests, our truck began to overheat. The downhill sections gave the truck a rest but with each climb the temperature gauge climbed as well. More than halfway to Lusaka and unable to turn back, we prayed the truck would make it over the last hill. A few times, we stopped at the top of an overpass to let the truck rest and feed it water. And, it would seem okay until the next climb. Finally, as we inched toward the top of a particularly large hill, the engine blew its head gasket. We were at a dead stop.

The constant stops had slowed us so much that the sun was setting as our truck gave up the ghost. We were like Mark, strolling behind the schoolhouse, unable to see the dangers lurking in the foliage. Unlike Mark, we were watchful, knowing that what we couldn't see might kill us.

As we waited, I don't remember being afraid to die. I was only afraid of being hurt before I died. As with mambas and cobras, the guerillas were more frightening for the pain they would inflict than for the death they could bring. In Zambia, death was inevitable, pain was avoidable.

I don't know how long we'd been sitting in the dark and watching the trees when a jeep drew up behind us. Two men with machine guns stepped out from the vehicle and walked up alongside our truck.

As the two guards stood still, machine guns at the ready, another man climbed out of the jeep and walked toward my father's window. Dad rolled down his window and looked at the man's official-looking uniform. I think I held my breath. This time, there was no calling for sticks and shovels.

The man gave Dad an incredulous look, eyebrows furled, mouth just barely smiling, and said, "Do you know this is guerilla territory?"

Dad said, "Yes," and explained the situation. He finished with, "We hadn't intended to be in the area after dark, but we couldn't have planned on the lorry breaking down."

It turned out the man was a Zambian military officer, looking for military deserters who'd been spotted in the area. He offered to tow us to the next town, where his brother owned a garage, and where we could get a place to stay. He also stated the obvious, "You're lucky I found you before someone else did."

And so, we had another story to tell at the Thanksgiving table. Like Mark's puff adder, the guerillas had been too slow to strike us in the night. Like Martha's mamba, death had been close but had slithered back into the trees. Like the people who came running with sticks and shovels, our Zambian officer had chased the snakes away. In time, we'd even laugh at the question the officer had asked, "Do you know this is guerilla territory?" As if we hadn't grown up there. As if we were happy tourists, blithely unaware of the dangers in the grass.

Other types of historic events can also impact the MK's development. One such example is when technological advancements impact the distribution of information. One generation of MKs may have little or at best restricted contact with extended family within the passport country, then the advancement and access to electronic mail means that the next generation of MKs has the potential for daily access to communication with extended family. One generation of MKs may not have access to information about social changes within the passport country and then the next generation of MKs has ready access to multi-media that facilitates up to the minute access to social changes. Historic events, advancements, social or political deterioration may not directly impact the MK and yet they influence choices available within the span of childhood both to the MK and on behalf of the MK. They therefore, need to be accounted for as factors of significance in the total make-up of the MK developmental ecology, factors that ultimately lead to adult outcomes.

In some instances, the MK may be very aware of enhanced or restricted available options but in some cases, these are not acknowledged until the maturity of adult reflection alerts the adult MK to their significance.

Increased social restrictions…Rosalea as a young adult

Mountain climbing was a favorite recreation activity during my teenage years. The highlands of Papua New Guinea are made up of many mountain ranges, one summit connecting to the next range. Some of the heights could be conquered in a day, starting early and getting back down again in the late afternoon. During my teens the school organized regular climbs and we were taught some map reading skills. Mostly the benefit was in breathing the cool fresh air and keeping up a hiking pace throughout the day.

The Church youth group leaders were less worried about map reading skills when they took us mountain climbing. Some of the Mission Aviation Fellowship pilots who led our youth group would circle their planes over the ranges and pick one not too far out of town that we could climb and then end the day with a swim in a river at the base. It was not an exact science and sometimes the mountain we climbed wasn't the one they thought they had chosen. There was one occasion when we were supposed to climb up and over a mountain to be collected by our parents at a river at the base on the other side. Unfortunately, we came down on the same side of the mountain as we had gone up. There were some worried parents late that afternoon!

Sometimes we didn't climb mountains. Instead, we straddled inflated inner tubes of tires from heavy machinery and caught the currents of the fast-flowing mountain rivers. We wore long pants and shoes to protect our legs from the sharp rocks that shaped the currents of these mountainous waters. I preferred the mountain climbing.

Wilhelm is the highest peak in PNG, reaching some 15,000 feet above sea level. I didn't climb that in my teens but I did make the hike to the top when I went back to visit my parents after I finished university. It was exhilarating to breathe the fresh mountain air and to feel the pumping in my chest from keeping pace with other hikers when the gradient was steep. I swam in the cool mountain water of the lake outside the base camp the evening I got back from the climb to the summit. The smells and sensations of home were good for the soul after the years in my passport country.

My early years in PNG had allowed the scope to enjoy the outdoors. PNG is a beautiful island country in the Pacific. The people I'd grown up amongst had been accepting and generous. As the years had passed and educated but unemployed young people filled the towns, it had become less carefree. I wasn't allowed to walk about town by myself. An expatriate woman had been grabbed and her jaw had been broken by gang members while walking through the golf course. PNG's transition to self-governance had not been a smooth journey. The economy struggled and people were disillusioned with their education that did not lead to jobs. They couldn't go back to village life, it was a culture to which they no longer belonged. And tribalism was an issue that seemed insurmountable. Achieving true democracy is a challenge in any country, but more so where there are more than 700 language groups represented within one country of three million people.

PNG was no longer the carefree paradise it had once been. I was grateful for the memories and for the era of PNG's history that had given me such a childhood. That place no longer existed for the university graduate who sat watching the sun set below the ranges that surrounded the base camp of Mt. Wilhelm.

Time is recognized as a factor of significance in child development.[3] This includes both the timing of significant personal and family events and the accumulation of events over time. The age of the child at the time of a significant personal or family incident affects the degree of impact on the child. This can include such things as the birth of a sibling, the experience of a shared family vacation, separation from or the death of a loved one. The MK has no control over these things and yet they impact the ecology within which he or she matures. For example, when a sibling is born after the MK has gone to boarding school, it may be more difficult for the two children to develop a familial bond. A shared family vacation at a time when the MK is particularly processing his or her identity may become a reference point for the rest of his or her childhood. The timing of events can seldom be adequately contrived and yet this backdrop to childhood is significant.

The accumulation of events is another important dimension to the element of time. An MK who is born after the parents have become missionaries is raised, fully immersed within the ecology. If the MK enters the ecology at some point during childhood then there is a necessary period of adjustment. If the MK is young this will probably be less of an adjustment than if the MK is older and can cognitively and intentionally process the transition. The length of time spent within the MK ecology differs for each child and the accumulation of events in his or her life is directly proportional to that period of time. At this stage there is no supporting research upon which to draw, however, it could be assumed that the longer the period of time spent as an MK as well as the ages at which the MK ecology is entered and exited could all affect the depth of impact on the developing child. The strength of related adult character traits could be in proportion to the amount of time spent in the MK ecology and the timing of entry and exit from it. MK specific research is not available to validate this assumption but documentation about child development in general supports the assumption of the impact of timing both in terms of the occurrence of specific events and the accumulation of events.

> The strength of related adult character
> traits could be in proportion to the amount
> of time spent in the MK ecology and the
> timing of entry and exit from it.

The God-factor and the related adult outcomes have been described earlier in this book. Circle "D" incorporates this significant factor in the MK developmental ecology. Everything that happens in the life of the MK is referenced by the fact that he or she is growing up abroad for the singular purpose of fulfilling the Great Commission as mandated by Christ in the biblical book of Matthew. In some instances, the MK families are engaged in works of development or humanitarian aid. In some cases where there is restricted access to a given country, missionaries seek secular employment within the country or teach English or other skills, or work in any number of divergent activities so as to live amongst those who need a living witness of God's love for them. In every case the MK is an MK because of a response to the command to go and take the message about Christ to those who need to hear it.

Whether it is covert or overt, an MK is an MK because of the God of the Christian faith. In every case, the MK lives with the God-factor as a backdrop upon which his or her childhood is painted. The God-factor impacts choices a family will make about life-style, social engagement, religious tolerance, educational opportunities for the child, and priorities in life. The God-factor determines the length of time a child is immersed in the MK ecology because of the response of adults to the call of God to go and live amongst those who need to hear about Christ. The God-factor determines the foundation and the final word upon which answers are drawn when the MK poses questions about big and small issues in life.

Although it is acknowledged as a backdrop to childhood, the God-factor is so powerful that it becomes, over time, perhaps the most significant element of the MK psyche and adult identity. Adult MKs can seldom talk about their childhood experiences without acknowledging the power of the God-factor on whom they have become. If they have developed an identity based upon an authentic and comprehensive understanding of a God they perceive as reasonable, then the acknowledgement will be positive. If however, there is unresolved resentment at what had to be sacrificed in childhood or disappointment over priorities the MK did not agree with during his or her childhood then the reflections about the God-factor will be less than positive and in fact sometimes hostile. The God-factor is indeed, a significant factor in the MK developmental ecology.

> The God-factor is so powerful that it
> becomes, over time, perhaps the most
> significant element of the MK psyche
> and adult identity.

Having explored the outcomes of the MK ecology and traced them back to factors in the childhood that directly lead to the adult outcomes the next section of the book will be devoted to a description of specific things that can be done to constructively intervene in the developmental ecology. This will be followed by a discussion of ways to interact with adult MKs with reference to their unique adult traits.

Part 3: What now?

Chapter 8: Intervention into the MK ecology

Intervention: Who Should Do This?

The term intervention encompasses any deliberate action that is taken to impact an outcome. In years gone by many missionaries and mission agency personnel were not aware that there would be such distinctly recognizable adult traits as a result of an MK childhood. The growing body of research and carefully recorded personal reflections that are now available provide an ever-deepening understanding of the impact of the MK experience. It is possible now to reliably establish some deliberate actions or intervention that will enhance the richness of the MK experience and protect against potential vulnerability.

This book has established areas of both enrichment and potential vulnerability in the developmental ecology of the MK. It has also identified people who are influential within the MK ecology. God has the interests of MKs as a high priority and He works through human agents to help Him to respond to this high priority.

> God has the interests of MKs as a high priority and He works through human agents to help Him to respond to this high priority.

The graphic description of the MK ecology (Figure 2.2) shows the broadening layers of influence around the MK. Chapters six and seven describe the specific dyadic relationships within which the MK engages during childhood and the social development that takes place within those relationships. The adults who play a significant role in shaping the life of the MK are the ones who hold the power to offer constructive intervention within the MK ecology. These adults can take deliberate action that will help the MK absorb the richness of the experiences of his or her childhood and at the same time help the MK develop life skills to manage the areas of potential vulnerability.

Influential adults include: parents, teachers, other missionaries, personnel from the home office of the mission agency, host country nationals who work with or befriend the family, and other expatriates living in the same location. These are adults of significant influence who can help the MK to grow in self-awareness, social capacity, and spiritual understanding. When influential adults commit themselves to deliberate action to impact the outcome of the MK experience in these three areas this is the most constructive intervention that can be applied within the MK ecology.

Self-Awareness

Self-awareness empowers a person. Self-awareness means having a keen understanding of one's strengths, limitations, motives, and values.[1] People grow in these areas as they mature. However, those who are taught the skills of regular self-reflection and thoughtfulness will be more likely to develop a heightened capacity of self-awareness. Figure 2.2 placed the MK, self, at the center of the developmental ecology. Self brings to the ecology strengths, weaknesses, social and anti-social orientation. Self interacts with all the other elements of the ecology according to God-given personality traits as well as personal qualities that may have been developed in a different context before the child became an MK. An MK who is encouraged to take the time to thoughtfully reflect on his or her own strengths and limitations, values and motives, will be better equipped to respond to the MK experiences in an informed manner. This is not to encourage the child to be self-centered or to see strengths and limitations as an excuse for inappropriate responses within the MK ecology but rather it is thoughtful reflection for the purpose of self-management.

*Self in the MK ecology…*Rosalea as a child

"She tends to dominate her sister." I felt a knot form in my stomach as I thought about the suggestion that I did not always act in the best interest of my older sister. The words were written on a page not meant for my eyes. It had been carelessly left on a table and I had begun to read when I had spotted my name. I went on to read carefully chosen words that further described my somewhat aggressive tendencies that served to overshadow my gentler sister. I wondered if anyone had tried to tell me these things about myself and whether I had just chosen not to listen or to receive the information. The knot in my stomach grew and my throat began to constrict because I was loyal, to a fault, to my older sister. I would protect her from anyone or anything. I felt very sad that I might be perceived to be hurtful to her in anyway.

This was the beginning of some self-examination for me. How could I behave better and bring out the best in my sister? I wondered if someone had tried to show me that in the past and I had not listened or received the information.

When you live away from home you need each other. We'd spent the past three years living in boarding homes during the school term and last year we'd been in two different towns, my sister in one boarding home and me in another. This year we were back together and this would be the year that I would learn to temper my tendencies. I didn't know if it was possible but I was determined to try. I was 11 years old and I wanted to be a better person for my sister as we managed our shared, unusual life.

Influential adults can teach the MK to ask questions such as: What is important to me? Who is important to me? Do I feel comfortable in this setting? Why or why not? Do I feel competent to do this thing? Some children can articulate clear responses to such questions from an early age, some need to be coached and guided in their reflection. Once an MK responds to such questions then he or she can grow in self-management.

Adults who have not developed self-awareness themselves will not be confident or competent in guiding MKs in this area. The first thing an influential adult who wants to offer constructive intervention in the MK ecology of development needs to do is to choose to grow in self-awareness and self-management himself or herself. Adults serious about such a commitment to MKs can make use of commercial tests that help to establish a person's profile traits. Such tools help the adult to honestly acknowledge strengths, limitations, values, and motives if they are administered and then individuals are given opportunity to engage in honest dialogue about the outcomes. Many mission agencies make use of such instruments to evaluate missionary candidates before approving them for ministry so they have access to them to extend to broader purposes. Some of these instruments have been validated for use with young people[2] and so could be administered to adults and to teens. Personnel within mission agencies could advocate for the use of such tools, accompanied by follow-up dialogue, as a deliberate action that represents constructive intervention into the MK ecology.

Managing Self Within the Ecology: Knowing the Developmental Ecology

Self-management of course, requires that the MK grow in awareness of the uniqueness of the developmental ecology within which his or her childhood unfolds. To manage oneself, one needs to know what significant elements exist within the ecology that therefore need to be negotiated during childhood. This allows the child to anticipate things that will be encountered. Influential adults can converse with the child about high mobility, the regular turnover of friendships, the colorfulness of social patterns within each of the countries of residence, the exposure to people of multiple countries, the God-factor, and the connection to the mission system. These topics naturally arise but the influential adult can intervene and establish a constructive glossary that permits the MK to enter into honest and open dialogue that then leads to increased self-awareness and maturing self-management.

Influential adults play a significant role in guiding self-management. Human nature instinctively chooses self-protection over exposure to risk. It is in this instinctive pattern of behavior that MKs gradually nurture the adult traits that are potentially challenging. Influential adults hold the power to take deliberate action, intervene, and help the MK to choose to grow in areas that can be difficult. This is self-management. If trusted adults intervene they have the power to provide safe, affirming contexts that allow the MK to explore alternative behavior patterns during childhood so that there are fewer potential challenges in the adult profile of the MK.

> Influential adults hold the power to
> take deliberate action, intervene, and
> help the MK to choose to grow in areas
> that can be difficult.

For example, the high mobility of childhood and the affinity with at least two different countries potentially leads to a diminished sense of belonging in any place or with any one group of people (Table 3.1). An influential adult will establish a glossary that affirms respect for the values and established social functions of both a passport country and host country or countries. The MK will absorb the concept that one does not need to establish loyalty with one country to the exclusion of another. During periods of painful separation from the friends or family in one location or another, the MK will be less likely to express negative feelings about the immediate location. An MK who has to remove himself or herself from a valued friendship group formed in the host country so that the missionary family can travel in the passport country for a period of time can be so resentful of the separation that he or she may see little of value in the passport country. Influential adults guide the reflections of the MK by affirming the pain of separation from friends while also affirming the relationship with people in the passport country who support the missionary family so they can continue the work abroad. While allowing open and honest dialogue, using the constructive glossary that is meaningful to the MK, the impact of high mobility is acknowledged as is the affinity with more than one country. Gradually the MK is guided in determining whether a sense of belonging is with people, within a location of residence, or perhaps a synthesis of the two. The MK's self-awareness is heightened as he or she explores the reasoning of the pain caused by social separation, and grows in self-management as he or she is offered a safe and affirming relationship to explore a response to the unique elements of his or her childhood.

Running away…Dina reflecting as an adult

When I was 15 my parents had to go back to the States for three months to raise some support. From the age of five we had only been back to the States twice (in 1st grade and 6th grade). My parents were excited as they planned the trip, saying, "We're going to get to go home for a few months!" I was beside myself. Home was right here where we were, not over there. We were just going into the summer months in Peru, my favorite time! Going to the States meant we would be facing bitter cold and snow in Indiana. I'd also have to spend time making new friends all over again and talking to people who were "family" by blood relation, but I really had no clue who they were. I was so distraught, I developed a plan to run away. I felt like nothing was in my control so I decided to take matters into my own hands. The night before we were supposed to fly out to the USA, I waited until everyone in the family had gone to sleep and then snuck out of the house, climbed over the 8 ft hedge around it and slipped into the streets of Lima. My plan was simple, I'd simply disappear long enough for my family to leave for the States. Then I'd spend the summer with friends and I'd reunite with my family when they returned in 3 months. I just simply didn't want to go to that place called "home" that wasn't home.

Thankfully, the Holy Spirit woke my mom up shortly after I left and persuaded her to go check my room. My whole family got in the car in the middle of the night and began searching for me. They finally found me just a few hours before our flight was scheduled to leave Lima. At the time I was chagrined and felt condemned to spending three months in the USA but looking back I'm thankful they found me because who knows what could have happened to me in the streets of a city of seven million people?

Managing Self Within the Ecology: Identity Construction

Establishing a personal, autonomous, sense of identity is one of the developmental tasks of childhood. This can be a challenging process for the MK who has to reconcile identity within multiple locations and within multiple and complex relationships. Influential adults can play a significant, intervening role in an MK's identity construction. However, these adults need to be open to supporting the MK if he or she chooses to explore alternative paths in the identity search process. This does not imply compromise of social or Christian fundamentals but it does necessitate openness on the part of influential adults to question their own prior assumptions in all areas of life in order to relevantly engage with the MK in the process of identity construction.

In identity construction, individuals answer the questions: Who am I? and Why am I who I am? Every individual will answer this question within his or her mind. When filling in forms we answer it with words that define legal nationality, birth country, gender, marital status, and home address. The confines of such forms can generate agitation for the MK for whom a personalized sense of identity incorporates much more than these basic elements. In some cases, the agitation arises because there is more than one answer and to respond with one is to deny another. For example, home address for the MK may mean physical locations on two different continents. To the pragmatist this seems trivial when a form simply requires a mailing address to receive information. However, to the MK who holds an internal affinity with at least two national groups, something that is understood by very few in his or her life, these small things challenge a valued component of his or her identity.

> In identity construction, individuals
> answer the questions: Who am I?
> and Why am I who I am?

Influential adults can help MKs, during childhood to identify which parts of their individualized identities are important to them and explore how each element can be appropriately manifested in the maturing identity. Obviously filling in a form with two different addresses will not satisfy the need to retain loyalty to a country of one's childhood and a passport country. However, opportunity to represent the affinity with a childhood country even when living elsewhere can be a way to appropriately manifest this important part of the MK's identity. Some MKs wear tokens gathered in their childhood country, or display maps, pictures, or artifacts in their physical place of residence. Some MKs choose to abstain from engaging in patriotic activities that signal an allegiance to only one country. If influential adults guide and support these conscious choices while the MK matures then the MK can learn to manifest them appropriately as part of his or her identity construct, rather than in a covert or often misunderstood manner in adult life.

Nomads…Lindsay reflecting as an adult

I am married to an adult MK. When we took our vows I never thought of that as a significant factor in our relationship. In my mind, Rosalea was really just a fun-loving country girl with the intriguing ability to make home-made bread from scratch. Well, she was always more than that! But my understanding of the impact of her life's experience upon her adult character was about that deep. It has taken me many years to recognize some of the profound threads in Rosalea's character that tie her to her childhood years.

I am an Australian, and like some other Australians, my upbringing had been mildly nomadic. I lived on a farm until I was 10 years old but once that farm was sold my family and I progressed through a number of different houses before I finished school. After school I took on a nomadic life of my own. Between the ages of 17 and 23 I held more than twenty different jobs and stayed in too many different trailer parks to remember. When I was almost twenty-four, I found Christ, and life changed dramatically. I enrolled at Bible College and for the first time since I was 10 years old, I stayed in one place for a full four years. When I met Rosalea, I figured that her nomadic upbringing was remarkably similar to mine. This was confirmed by the ease with which we formed a deep friendship.

In retrospect, she did have some strange habits though! Sometimes she used words incorrectly (to my mind) and she had odd pronunciation for some other words. I was amazed to find out that she did not know some of the television shows that I grew up watching and I teased Rosalea about her lack of exposure.

Some issues were a little more serious though. As we approached our marriage, she used to joke that I would someday leave her too; just occasionally that was more insulting than funny. After we were married and moved into the pastorate, I started to notice that she adopted a different tone of voice, almost a formal tone, when speaking to particular people. That tone of voice gave me the impression that she was pretending to be someone different when trying to be a "proper pastor's wife." I did wonder at times why Rosalea couldn't just relax and be herself.

One year after our marriage, I graduated from Bible College and we moved into the pastorate. Two years later we were finally able to visit Rosalea's childhood home in the highlands of Papua New Guinea. It was an amazing three-week visit to several remote stations. We landed on a narrow airstrip in a tiny airplane, stayed in the houses where Rosalea grew up, hiked up mountains, drank out of bamboo water-bottles, and sat and talked with local pastors who had known her as a child. It was the first time I had really heard Rosalea speaking fluently in

Pidgin English. I began to recognize some of the places and the people that she and her family spoke about. Just the same, I still did not really understand how profoundly different her upbringing was to my own.

We served in the pastorate for some years before going to the mission field in Africa ourselves. As our two sons began to grow up, I found myself trying to educate them about the same silly television characters about which I used to tease Rosalea. I found myself adopting different words and pronunciations for ease of communication in our multi-cultural setting. Gradually I began to recognize some of the fundamental differences between our two childhoods.

Perhaps the most distinct realization came when we were in Mozambique and attended an international church. Some comment was made about the distinctive character of Australians. I remember remarking to Rosalea that, despite our years overseas, I was still as much an Aussie as anyone that I had ever met. I was raised in rural Australia under real Aussie parents. I had worked in the Outback, shot and eaten kangaroos, fished on the Great Barrier Reef, worked on construction sites and drunk in the pubs. In my heart of hearts, I have an unshakable identity. I am an Aussie, regardless of where you meet me. In contrast, when asked about her nationality, Rosalea would comment cryptically that she carried an Australian passport.

Our MK sons, despite being born in the same hospital as I had been born, knew very little of the Aussie life. They carried Australian passports, but I had to explain to them who Captain Cook was. One had a British flavor to his accent and the other had an American flavor. They understood about poverty and airplanes and exchange rates, but they didn't know the poetry of Banjo Paterson. I came to understand that, although we were a family of nomads, there was at least one fundamental difference between us; I always knew where my home was. That confidence goes with me wherever I go.

At the same time, I see that our sons have a different confidence. At six or seven years old they regularly held meaningful and extended conversations with adults and at thirteen they could get on a plane alone and travel away from home for weeks without noticeable stress. As teenagers they have already chosen to be baptized and they have plans for their future education and career/ministries. My nomadic youth was an aimless wandering, but our sons have a far deeper awareness of a purposeful life than I did at the same age.

Over the years Rosalea and I have both come to understand her MK heritage. Somewhere along the path she stopped using her formal tone of voice and she stopped thinking that I was going to leave her. She is stuck with me, for better or for worse. Today we have raised two MK sons, who hopefully have a better understanding of their own rich and unique upbringing because of the issues that we have faced together.

A sense of ease about one's identity is a strong foundation for adult life choices. An MK who is guided and supported through the search to construct and be confident in his or her identity, even when it does not make sense to the majority of people around him or her will make more reasoned life choices as an adult. Sometimes influential adults can make extreme efforts to retain a connection with the passport country and this may become a pressure on the MK to absorb exclusive patriotism to the passport country. An MK who has pressure from influential adults to conform to a prescribed mold, may make extreme or rebellious choices in adult life.

Managing Self Within the Ecology: Managing the Extremes

Sometimes the distinctives of the developmental ecology are glorified for the MK and the result can be a superficial sense of status or importance. An alternative response can be resentment that the reality of the impact of those distinctives was denied or minimized.

If influential adults speak to the MK only of the breadth of friendships he or she has formed with people from many different nationalities, without also acknowledging the fact that the child had little opportunity to form enduring childhood friendships, then reality has been denied or minimized.

The MK may not feel at liberty to grieve the lost friendships or to be honest about how difficult it is to become intimate with people in adulthood because of the abbreviated and truncated relationships during childhood. If, however, influential adults help the child to establish and use a vocabulary that allows the healthy expression of grief along with a vocabulary that describes how to retain continuous communication with the breadth of friends made during childhood, then the distinctives of the ecology are normalized. Such intervention is constructive. The child is given opportunity to grow in self-awareness and mature in self-management skills.

Sometimes extreme choices are made on behalf of the MK during developmental years and these are difficult for any concerned adult or peer to explain to the MK either as a child or during reflection in adult life. Sometimes an MK has a particular disposition that struggles with a given context, reaches a challenging age, or begins to manifest attention seeking behaviors that are overlooked by those adults who are responsible for the child. No amount of coaching in self-awareness can make up for the fact that this child needs additional care and nurture. If this is not provided and the child is left to cope with the extreme or challenging context, then there will be long-term pain for the individual as well as for those who try to establish intimate relationships with him or her in adult life. In such instances there is no way to normalize the MK ecology of development. The distinctives accentuate troubling childhood years. Such situations demand extreme decisions that will ensure that the MK is reassured that he or she is the most important product of the missionary family.

Social Maturity: Age Equivalent Dyadic Relationships

Constructive intervention is needed throughout childhood so that the MK learns healthy social behaviors. Influential adults have a role to play in facilitating healthy dyadic relationships for the MK. If the MK is engaged in a number of appropriate and enduring dyadic relationships during childhood, then there will be greater opportunity for enriched social development. Influential adults are responsible to facilitate these relationships. This needs to be both with age equivalent peers and with adults. Healthy and enduring dyads provide the MK with opportunity to experience controlled shifts in power over time, healthy conflict management, the acquisition of healthy grieving patterns, and a belief in the continuity of long-term relationships of significance.

> Healthy and enduring dyads provide
> the MK with opportunity to experience
> controlled shifts in power over time.

The pattern of heightened mobility during childhood is one with which the MK must live. Mobility is a fact of life for MKs. For some there is much greater mobility than for others, however, it is a factor of significance for all MKs. Therefore, the turnover of people in the MK's life will also continue to be an issue. With this as a given, adults of influence can determine ways to establish and retain a special connection between the MK and certain other people. For example, if an MK has a close friend within the host country then the parents can explore ways to retain the communication and connection between the two children while the MK is in the passport country for any length of time. Electronic mail can be used in some cases. In other instances, there may be the opportunity for the two children to exchange letters or small gifts in the post. Children cannot manage such a connection alone. Adults need to be aware of the importance of such communication that will help to facilitate a smoother transition back into the disrupted social network from which the MK has been withdrawn.

In some cases, a missionary is closely bonded to a sibling or friend in the passport country and can use this relationship to help the MK establish an enduring dyad. If the sibling or friend has children then the missionary can find ways to facilitate communication and connection between the MK and the other child or children. The more consistent age equivalent peers the MK has during childhood, the greater the chance of establishing healthy behavior patterns to carry into adult life. Parents cannot contrive friendships for their children but they can act as constructive facilitators that allow friendships to grow and to endure. This is a constructive intervention parents can have into the MK ecology.

Social Maturity: Dyadic Relationships with Adults

The importance of non-familial adults in the social development of the child has been described earlier in this book. Parents have a role to play in helping MKs wisely determine which adult relationships to pursue and which ones to avoid. Some adults will not contribute to the healthy development of a child and parents play the role of protector for their children against such adults. This is true no matter where the child is raised. There are other adults who can become role models and friends to particular children and these are the ones with whom an MK needs to forge healthy and enduring dyadic relationships.

A dyad is a relationship between two people where each member remains in the thought of the other even when the two are separated. A dyadic relationship between an MK and a non-familial adult who has chosen to befriend that child is one of the most powerful relationships within the MK ecology. Parents and siblings share powerful relationships for the child because the unusual missionary life is a shared journey. Family values are instilled in the child and the family bond can be strong. However, the non-familial adult who has singled out the MK and chosen to engage in a relationship with that child also has considerable power to shape his or her values and life choices. The fact that the relationship is chosen is where the power resides. For many MKs this is experienced within the mission agency system.

> The fact that the relationship is
> chosen is where the power resides.

Other adult missionaries befriend the child and help the family to nurture the MK. The absence of extended family adds further strength to these relationships. Other missionary families are witness to the milestones and cycles of life that the MK experiences. Occasions normally shared with extended family, such as Christmas, birthdays, and graduations, are shared with other missionary families. Births, deaths, baptisms, the loss of a first tooth, leaving for boarding school, and a long list of other events that mark the trajectory of life are witnessed and shared by other missionary families. The joy and the pain of life becomes a shared history.

The shared history is inevitable where missionaries share a location. However, the deliberate choice to nurture a dyadic relationship with a child is not inevitable. As influential adults are made aware of the power of such relationships they can commit to these relationships as a constructive intervention. Influential adults can choose to spend time with an MK, choose to teach an MK a skill in which he or she expresses a particular interest, acknowledge birthdays and special events important to the MK, and most significantly commit to pray for and with that chosen MK. Parents who are aware of a chosen relationship can facilitate its emergence by inviting that adult to spend time with the family, helping the MK to reciprocate in communication or gift exchanges for special occasions and dialogue with the MK about the importance of the relationship.

Sometimes chosen adult dyadic relationships are formed with teachers, other expatriates, and host country nationals, especially those closely associated with the work within which missionaries are engaged. Wherever these are formed parents need to act as protector of the MK so that safe boundaries are established. An MK will not necessarily recognize contexts where he or she can be preyed upon.

Within safe dyadic relationships the MK has the potential to learn the gradual shift in power that establishes social maturity.[3] Within these powerful dyads the MK can build self-definition and establish a healthy sense of self-worth. While the MK is young the adult in the relationship has the advantage of age and experience but over time these factors are balanced out as the adult guides the MK into appropriate assertiveness of his or her own identity within the relationship. The balance of power shifts gradually until such time as the adult and the MK eventually emerge as mature friends. The influential adult within the dyad has helped to guide the MK into social maturity. It is within such a relationship that the MK can learn that it is possible to trust others and to be appropriately vulnerable with another person. The excessive turn-over of relationships within the MK ecology naturally leads the MK to establish patterns of self-protection within relationships. However, enduring dyadic relationships wherein the MK feels safe and willing to trust and be vulnerable, reinforces the acceptance that relationships are worth an investment. A commitment to an enduring chosen dyadic relationship with an MK is a powerful, constructive intervention that has the potential to impact adult relational patterns for that MK.

Spiritual Growth: Christian Disciplines

The God-factor has been highlighted in this book as a significant element of the MK developmental ecology. In order to maximize the benefit of early and extreme exposure to spirituality the MK needs strong and relevant Christian discipleship. Christian discipleship is essential for any child so it is not presented here as a unique need for the MK but rather it is presented as an area that requires deliberate intervention on the part of influential adults in order to impact MK adult outcomes.

Missionaries are usually spiritually mature Christians who have followed the call of God to the point of sacrifice in order to fulfill the Great Commission. MKs usually grow-up surrounded by adults who are in the habit of regularly reading the Bible and praying, participating in group worship, tithing, and giving sacrificially. These spiritual disciplines are modeled within the family and by those who most closely associate with the MK. It is easy for the MK to learn the value of these Christian practices. Most missionaries are also aware of their need to be growing in grace and wisdom as Christian believers. Sometimes, however, missionary families are placed in a given location and required to cooperate in work assignments with others with whom they do not easily relate. MKs can be close witness to some ungracious behavior when there is unresolved tension between missionaries. Observation of these relationships also impacts the development of the MK. The role modeling of influential adults in the life of the MK needs to be consistent in order for the MK to develop a healthy and comprehensive understanding of God.

Social Maturity: Relevant Discipleship

The Christian discipleship of MKs also needs to be relevant. Many things taught in the Bible are Christian principles rather than mandates to which one must adhere. Some of the Bible is universal in its application but there are many parts that may be applied differently in one social context than in another. Sensitive missionaries allow that the host country nationals may manifest holiness in a very different, socially acceptable way than the people from his or her passport country. However, missionaries can find it challenging if an MK explores a socially alternative way of manifesting a heart that is totally surrendered to God.

MKs hear the preaching of God's truths in at least two different, socially diverse locations and they witness the application of those same truths in both those locations. The MK belongs entirely to neither culture and yet has competencies to negotiate both. It creates inner turmoil for the MK to try to conform to the social norms of either group of people. When God's truths are applied to social conduct this inner turmoil is heightened for the MK.

Strong and relevant discipleship needs to focus on the character of God. The MK needs to be discipled into a deep understanding of God that then leads to a hunger for a close relationship with Him. The manifestation of godliness and its social application is then built upon personal conviction. Personal conviction of how to represent one's total surrender to God grows out of an ever-maturing sensitivity to the guidance of the Holy Spirit.

> The MK needs to be discipled into a deep
> understanding of God that then leads to a
> hunger for a close relationship with Him.

Families have norms and spiritual practices, as do mission agencies, and national churches. The MK is exposed to these throughout childhood. Sensitive adults do not deny these surrounding norms however, they do allow MKs the freedom to explore personal application of their emerging love of God. Constructive intervention is to acknowledge the God-factor in the life of the MK and then to support the MK in a discovery of the depth of God's character. Influential adults who would choose to competently achieve such helpful intervention must take stock of their own prior assumptions about God's character. Influential adults must honestly evaluate their own personal assumptions about how godliness is manifested in order to determine whether these assumptions have been influenced more by accepted social norms than biblical principles.

Each individual must stand before God and give an account for his or her own days. Each MK needs to be discipled in a strong and relevant manner such that he or she can unreservedly give an account for a Christian life that was lived out based upon personal convictions guided by the voice of the Holy Spirit.

The care and well-being of MKs is a high priority. They are the first disciples of those called to live abroad in order to fulfill the Great Commission. MKs need to be nurtured and discipled throughout their childhood years. Once they become adults, they benefit from close relationships and affirmation from those who understand the childhood ecology that so greatly impacted their adult profile. The following chapter explores some of the ways to enhance a relationship with MKs who are now adults.

Chapter 9: **Relating to the adult MK**

The Richness: Acknowledging Differences

Adult MKs are different. Their worldview is different to most of those around them, their values and motivations in life have been shaped differently to most of those around them, their life choices cannot always be rationally explained to those who surround them. The adult MK's response to the overall experience of his or her childhood may range from being unreservedly positive about the whole childhood experience, to being unreservedly resentful of the whole childhood experience. For many adult MKs an honest evaluation probably lies somewhere in between the two extremes.

*Resolving identity...*Juli reflecting as an adult

In my high school and early college years in the USA, I was surprised and somewhat uneasy that much of my identity still stemmed from my childhood experiences abroad. I continued to seek out relationships with other TCKs and feel confused sometimes in the current social mores of my small communities. My new relationships, the ones that felt most satisfying to me, were with TCKs, yet I had many friends who had not lived in another culture. As I look back, I see that I vacillated between trying to identify with the culture-at-large, for example, by learning about fashion trends and sports teams and nurturing another more hidden identity that watched the news and discussed international concerns with my father. These two identities were kept quite separate as a teen and early college student.

In the latter part of college, I began to strongly identify with my international roots and view the predominant mono-cultural perspectives as inferior, thus alienating myself from many. In addition to the ongoing issues of identity and relationship, I was constantly moving from one place to the other. In nine years, I lived in six states and twelve different homes. As a middle age adult, I have no "home" town to which to return with my family, but find home where my loved ones are currently living. My family continues to be quite mobile, my parents live in a house I never knew as a child and my siblings live in Tokyo, New York, Indiana and Hawaii. Yet I connect with home through shared memories and in small familiar objects that I see in their various houses.

Most adult MKs can acknowledge the positive impact that a cross-cultural childhood has had on his or her development, most recognize the confidence that has grown out of exposure to global travel and significant global issues from a young age, most are aware of their heightened capacity for empathy and tolerance of alternative perspectives on life because of their own childhood experiences. Adult MKs value their capacity to adapt even when they profess a desire to remain in one location rather than continuing the patterns of mobility in their adult life. Most can speak of the impact that early exposure to extreme Christian living has had on their spiritual development. Most adult MKs are aware of the richness of their MK legacy. This richness defines them and it is helpful if those who establish close relationships with them also understand these defining childhood experiences and their related adult outcomes.

This richness defines them.

How does a person of significance in the adult MK's life try to comprehend the childhood experiences that have shaped the MK into the person he or she has become? Such a comprehension and connection with an adult MK is built upon an acceptance and respect for the unique traits that define the adult MK, an ability to honor the symbols that represent the connection between the adult MK and his or her childhood, and a willingness to explore the territory of the adult MK's childhood. The connection is enhanced when there is a reciprocal willingness on the part of the adult MK to explore the childhood territory experienced by the significant other in his or her life in order to discover how childhood experiences have shaped this individual.

The Richness: Identity Securing Talisman

Symbols from childhood become very important to the adult MK. Tangible objects become a bridge to connect the adult MK with the childhood world that cannot be reclaimed. Some MKs have the option of taking up permanent residence within the country of their childhood but most are there only as dependents of their parents who are deployed to a given country for a season of work and are required to leave at some point. It can be a challenge for the MK to establish an independent legally recognized status within the childhood country. Most MKs move on to establish residency in a country other than their childhood country in their adult life. Therefore, any connection with the childhood country is an important link for the adult MK.

A significant person in the life of the adult MK can recognize these links with childhood in the form of such things as artifacts displayed around the home of the adult MK, tokens or symbols worn by the adult MK, maps and pictures of the childhood country, or pets named after places of significance during childhood. Adult MKs who want to declare their difference and their pride in their alternative identity will display these symbols prominently. Those who want to blend in will be less overt but will usually jealously guard their grip on items of significance.

A tangible object that holds a connection to childhood becomes an identity securing talisman[1] to the adult MK. There is obviously no magic within this talisman, but it does hold the power to preserve an identity treasured by the adult MK. Significant people in the life of the adult MK will respect and treasure these tangible objects out of honor and care for the adult MK. There is deep pain for the adult MK when those with whom he or she is supposed to be intimate in adult life give only passing acknowledgement of these symbols or even refuse to have treasured objects displayed within a shared home. Taken at face value these talismans can be regarded as gaudy or distasteful. However, adult MKs will seldom admit to the pain caused when such views are expressed because the importance of a given talisman is not easily conveyed.

Talisman... the power to preserve an
identity treasured by the adult MK.

*Treasuring a few possessions/talismans...*Juli reflecting as an adult

When I was in high school, my father returned to visit Papua New Guinea. He brought back with him some black bracelets which are made from the rubber rings used to securely seal oil barrels. My father had bought these at one of the markets where fresh fruit and vegetables are sold alongside traditional artifacts. The people of PNG collect these rubber rings for adornment, sometimes carefully carving ornate patterns into them.

Since that time, I have never been without three to seven of these bracelets on my right wrist. For some reason, these bracelets, which an Indian friend presumed to be black ivory, represent my history, my roots, my identity. And now, my children at the ages of twelve and nine, each wear two on their right wrist as well. These rings are not worth much fiscally but they mean the world to me and my kids.

The Richness: Visiting the Childhood Home

Sensitive adults who build relationships with the adult MK are open and encouraging of dialogue about the childhood experiences of the adult MK. They express openness to trying to comprehend the experiences that have shaped the individual and they express a willingness to accept the differences in worldview, value positions, and motivation behind choices made, even when these are not understood. The MK childhood can never be comprehensively conveyed however, poignant elements can be empathetically absorbed. A way to absorb in part is to accompany the adult MK on a trip back to the childhood location. To walk the soil and to meet the people who formed a part of the developmental ecology is a statement of acceptance of who the adult MK was as a child but it also provides an opportunity to see and feel some of the reality of the experience. As an adult MK rediscovers a childhood location, and as he or she reconnects with people of his or her childhood years, there is the potential for reflection and open dialogue about those childhood experiences as well as their impact on the adult profile of the MK.

For this to be a well-rounded experience the adult MK would benefit from time spent in the location where a person of significance spent his or her childhood. The relationship between the two adults will be enriched if there is reciprocal understanding of how location and people from childhood shaped the person each has become. Each of us is a product of our childhood years as well as our inherited traits. The adult MK and those with whom close relationships are formed grow in their level of mutual understanding as they recognize this truth. Although the adult MK may feel vastly different to the majority of those around him or her, it is significant to acknowledge and accept that there is richness and challenge resulting from the childhood experiences of every individual. In any relational partnership each individual brings the by-products of childhood, both enriched and challenged. The two people in the partnership need to contribute to building the bridges that will forge an enduring healthy relationship.

*Visiting home...*Phil reflecting as an adult

My wife, Karen and I visited Papua New Guinea in 1981, a year after we were married and then we took our children in 1992. The first trip was part of a pair; the year after that we went to the USA to see the (concrete) jungle where Karen had grown up, Jersey City. She is a TCK as well.

On the first trip we went to Wewak, Fugwa and Mt. Hagen. At Wewak, the Coopers, who had been my boarding hostel parents, were back filling in at the Brethren hostel for whoever had taken over from them. We stayed at the apartments where our family stayed when my youngest sister was born. I remember it was fairly expensive staying there and traveling on the Missionary Aviation Fellowship planes to Fugwa and out to Mt. Hagen because we didn't get discounted missionary rates. I wasn't a missionary anymore.

I had been a bit of a horror when I was a child living at the hostel. I remember that it was good to catch up with the Coopers and apologize for the grief I had caused them when I was a child and to let them see I hadn't turned out too bad after all. Another significant memory I have from that trip was going to the bank. While standing in the line waiting to be served I stepped backwards and when I turned around to apologize to the guy whose toes I had stood on I found that it was Michael Somare, who was Prime Minister for the first time back then.

Karen flew out to the Fugwa mission station and I went by truck with one of the missionaries, stopping at another mission compound for the night on the way. Out at Fugwa, Karen was able to accompany Fran, the missionary nurse on her clinic visits to some of the villages. She developed a stomach bug and had to get out of the vehicle to vomit. She remembers all the locals laughing at her, seeing this white woman vomiting.

I recall visiting the Fugwa market on the first visit. I needed a string for my bow. I found one and in the trade language of Pidgin asked the guy how much. He told me 40 toea (the equivalent of cents), which I handed over and he gave me the string. His friend, standing beside him, said to him in the local language, Huli, "Rich white guy. You should have charged him 4 kina (the equivalent of dollars)!" What he didn't count on was the fact that I could still remember enough Huli to understand what he was saying. I said to them (in Pidgin, I can't speak Huli, just hear it) that I thought the transaction had actually gone quite fairly.

The weather was quite bad when we flew out from Fugwa. The MAF pilot who flew us was not normally based in the highlands of PNG, where they fly by sight in the small Cessna planes. He had brought a plane over from Australia and for some reason he was sent to get us. Even when he had been based in PNG he was in the Sepik, so he wasn't very familiar with the Southern Highlands.

The weather forced us around towards Pangia and he was trying to find a gap in the clouds but he was flying straight towards a mountain that I knew to be Mt. Ialibu. You could only see the base of the mountain and I was about to say something to him about what I knew to be inside those clouds. Right at that moment he found a hole in the clouds and shot up through it, flying right over Alia, another one of our missions' stations. I pointed Alia out to Karen as we went over it. Once we got out of the cloud and he could recognize where he was again, he asked me, "What did you say that place was?" The Alia strip had been closed and it wasn't on his map.

On the second trip when we took our kids up to PNG, we went to Pt. Moresby where my parents were living and to Fugwa, where my sister and her family were working as missionaries. We didn't like Pt. Moresby much at all. It was the first time I had ever been out of the airport there that I remember. Security was a big issue by then and we couldn't handle being enclosed in the high cyclone wire fences. While we were there the town water supply was cut off for 36 hours. It had happened the week before we got there and Dad had filled up a few 44 gallon drums in case it happened again. Some of the neighbors came over and he gave them some emergency rations of water.

We flew to Tari by Air Niugini and my brother-in-law came out and drove us in to Fugwa. The kids really enjoyed the time there. It was a lot like our childhood on the station. They liked the freedom to roam around with my sister's kids and the local children. Fugwa was still safe at that time, although there was some tribal fighting brewing and there was a murder (the first one since way back when the missionaries first went there) the week after we left. I enjoyed playing basketball with some of the people I had grown up with. I played center because they were all shorter than me. Fugwa had the provincial champion girls' team made up mostly of the nurses and teachers there. The guys would be in charge of how the games were run but they managed to get these girls on their teams. One of the kids I had played with as a child was now the Principal of the Fugwa school.

There was a meeting during the week where the pastors came in to the Fugwa station. My brother-in-law got me to bring a greeting. Then they had a big discussion about whether I was "agali timbu" (big man) enough to have a "bung" (combined) meeting with all the churches on the Sunday so that I could speak. Eventually they decided they would but again I'm not sure how much of the conversation they knew I was following. The old timers especially were very happy to see us. They kept saying, "Is it Guriguri?" (the Huli pronunciation of my brother, Gregory's name). He must have lived there for longer than I did. Someone pointed out a lemon tree that Dad had planted and so because I was the eldest son and trees are handed down in families, I had the right to pick the lemons any time I wished. Someone else gave us a live chicken, which was fairly useless to us to take anywhere else so we had to eat it there. The head lopping off incident has been well rehearsed in our family and in my sister's family.

Taking the family up to my childhood home gave them a frame of reference for sharing the memories I had of my childhood and created some memories of their own from the places that had been significant to me as a child.

The Challenges: Ongoing Mobility

Some of the greatest challenges to the adult MK are: the tendency towards ongoing mobility, deeply ingrained relational self-protection, and reconciling the God-factor. These factors, which represent challenges to the adult MK, can also become challenges to those who relate closely to him or her. Some adult MKs would choose to burn their passports and never travel again after the high mobility experienced during childhood. However, these represent the minority. Some adult MKs have well defined lists of countries they hope to yet visit. Others actively seek employment abroad as soon as they complete their undergraduate degrees or gain some experience in a chosen profession. Others move house or rearrange the furniture to satisfy the passion for change. Ongoing mobility or planned travel is a part of life for most adult MKs. Those who have had more sedentary childhood years can be eager to travel as adults however, they seldom share the embedded urge that adult MKs possess.

Ongoing mobility or planned travel
is a part of life for most adult MKs.

One of the challenges of ongoing mobility in adult life is that it can be difficult for adult MKs to build up career and social capital. While it may not be a priority to the adult MK to accumulate stock or credibility in these two areas it can be a challenge to those who walk through life with them. A husband or wife will be similarly required to sacrifice career and social capital if the adult MK submits to the urge to keep moving locations. It can be exciting to experience life in many and varied places and it can feed the MK's addiction to new experiences but in each new location new relationships have to be established and credibility in the workplace once again has to be built in order to be eligible for promotion in one's chosen career. A track record of ongoing mobility can cause potential employers to question one's ability to work without conflict or distraction. Both the adult MK and his or her partner have to continually reassert their worth within a workplace and this can be challenging.

Ongoing mobility affects the children born into a family of an adult MK. Ongoing mobility means that the children of adult MKs also experience truncated relationships and have to continually establish themselves within new social networks. The legacy of ongoing mobility is then passed on to another generation. While this does not have to be a negative thing, it is something that people of significance in the life of the adult MK need to understand and then they can negotiate terms of compromise as they live and work with the adult MK. The urge toward ongoing mobility can be resolved if the adult MK chooses employment that includes some amount of travel. It can be satisfied if the adult MK establishes the practice of regularly setting aside some portion of his or her income so that he or she can afford annual holidays in new and different places.

The Challenges: Relational Self-protection

Having to negotiate such compromise can itself be a challenge for the adult MK. MKs learn friendship initiation skills because they are constantly meeting new people and having to enter new social networks. However, they become quite independent because of the demands involved in negotiating new and diverse contexts during their childhood years. Working within groups and trusting people at a level that requires vulnerability can be a challenge to the adult MK. The well-established relational self-protection that has helped the MK to survive childhood can determine the level of intimacy achieved within adult relationships.

One of the most painful residual affects for the adult MK, and those closest to him or her, to deal with is that of relational self-protection. Allowing oneself to be vulnerable to another person necessarily carries with it the potential for hurt. The MK has learned that, when entering a new context or relationship, it is best to be an observer for a period of time and learn the norms and expectations before fully engaging in a group or a relationship. To engage too quickly is to risk making foolish blunders that then carry a costly personal or social price. When one cares too much about a friendship and the equivalent value on the friendship is not reciprocated then there is pain for any child. The MK tests out the level of reciprocation in friendships throughout childhood and over time learns that it is less costly to enjoy shallower friendships and not to seek intimacy in a relationship.

Even when there is a mutual desire for a deeper friendship, MKs and those around them live with the knowledge that one or the other will soon move on and the chance for retaining a close relationship is minimal. Gradually MKs learn to live with this reality and may not feel there is any dimension of social life lost to them. However, the challenge becomes a reality to be dealt with in adult life when the MK seeks to establish intimate relationships with other adults. This reality can be most keenly felt within marriage relationships.

Within marriage or other intimate relationships there is a need for both partners to invest in the relationship. Friendship grows and matures as each partner trusts the other with more of himself or herself. Intimacy deepens as there is greater mutual reliance upon each other. Relationships grow over time if there is investment from each partner and if there is a willingness to resolve issues as they arise. Relationships grow as each partner honors the other with a willingness to support the development of individual potential and a willingness to invest in achieving the potential they have as partners in the relationship. However, any or all of these areas can be a challenge for the adult MK and therefore a challenge to those who walk through life with him or her.

> Intimacy deepens as there is
> greater mutual reliance upon
> each other.

Where does one start in addressing these challenges? Once again, the issues of self-awareness and self-management are significant to the life of the MK. Progress can be made in reversing trends of self-protection within relationships if the adult MK is first willing to increase in self-awareness and then gradually adopt behaviors of self-management. The adult MK is a product of his or her childhood experiences and yet is seldom aware of the depth of impact the life events and patterns of childhood have had on his or her instinctive adult behavior. Adult MKs and those who care most about them need to explore the outcomes of the MK experiences and trace them back to their childhood source. Open acknowledgement is a starting point in addressing this significant challenge. From this heightened awareness constructive steps can be identified that will help the adult MK and those closest to him or her to relate with greater intimacy. However, patterns that have been established during childhood are deeply embedded and cannot be reversed simply by choice. They take time to realign into relational patterns that are more accommodating of depth and intimacy.

Self-protection manifests differently in each individual. Some adult MKs struggle to verbally express their sincere feelings because of a fear of rejection. Some struggle with eye contact or extended periods of time with any one person. In almost every situation where the adult MK manifests self-protective behavior, it is borne from a need to be in control of how vulnerable he or she is with the other person. The self-protective behaviors provide barriers of safety behind which the adult MK can shelter. Within a marriage relationship there is an expectation of extreme vulnerability one with another. This can be very threatening for individuals who have enduring patterns of self-protection and there can be an instinctive reaction to hold back or to control more intimate encounters within marriage. These behaviors inflict pain on those who seek intimacy with the adult MK.

Establishing the specific self-protective behavior that is manifested and acknowledging its source helps the adult MK and those closest to him or her to begin a constructive path that allows trust to build over time. If both partners become aware of what makes the adult MK feel most vulnerable then additional care can be established in this area of relating. Consistency and faithfulness within the relationship allow the adult MK to learn that not all relationships come to an end and that sometimes the mutual desire for intimacy can lead to a depth of relationship that has not before been experienced. The husband or wife, or other person within the intimate relationship brings to the partnership patterns established in his or her childhood. These need to be explored and compared so that there is a mutual understanding, as both partners seek to establish new and shared relational patterns. Relationships grow in depth and maturity as both partners invest. There is no room for one or the other to hide behind outcomes of childhood experiences. In some instances, professional input is needed to overcome relational challenges but in most instances mature adults, willing to invest in each other can establish healthy and pleasurable partnerships as trust is built over time.

The Challenges: Managing the God-factor

God leads parents into missionary work and God offers a close relationship to each accompanying child. Some MKs accept this offer of a relationship with God during childhood years, some accept it later in life. Not all MKs follow their parents in their choice to be Christian. The reasons for this reality vary from individual to individual. The polarized responses to the God-factor of the MK experience range from anger and resentment that God would require a family to experience the extremes of missionary life in order to fulfill the Great Commission, to an unconditional acceptance that whatever God or the Church asked, one should do without question or reservation. Most adult MKs attest to a response that falls somewhere between the two extremes.

A healthy response to the God-factor of the MK childhood acknowledges that God works through committed Christian people to achieve the Great Commission but there is a human cost for each individual who is involved in this venture to bring the people of the world to God. God calls the parents to the task and the children accompany them wherever the specific assignment takes them. In cases where children love the MK life and competently negotiate the demands of the MK ecology there must still be a resolution of the God-factor, an acknowledgement of the reality that God is the reason for the MK life with all its accompanying joy and pain. In some cases, the children are much more reluctant to be involved in the missionary lifestyle and the cost of being an MK seems to be, or to have been, too high. Resolving the God-factor is much more of a challenge for these individuals. Whether it is during childhood or in adult life, the MK needs to be guided into an understanding that residual pain related to any MK experiences and an acceptance of a close relationship with God are not mutually exclusive. It is possible to love God with a totally surrendered heart and at the same time admit to pain that was caused by being an MK. It is possible to grow in an ever-deepening relationship with God and still ask why certain choices were made on one's behalf during childhood years or why traumatic things were experienced. To deny the pain or to withhold the honest questions is to limit a maturing relationship with God.

As Isaac followed his father down the mountain (Genesis 22:1-19), was he wondering if he could continue to trust his father and his God? The Bible records no conversation between

Abraham and Isaac, or any communication between God and Isaac at that point, and yet Isaac was at the very center of that scenario where Abraham was asked to trust God to provide. With his own emerging faith in God, was Isaac also being asked to trust God to provide and protect? The Bible does not elaborate on that point however, it does go on to describe the poignant elements of Isaac's own adult life and his growing devotion to the God of Abraham, who clearly became the God of Isaac. Could it be that Isaac was somehow able to reconcile the painful, God ordained experience of his youth with his own emerging understanding of God's character and call upon his life? A love and devotion to God was the mark of Isaac's life, as it had been upon Abraham's and later it was upon Jacob's.

Isaac's ability to reconcile the pain of his extreme experience and his growing love of God can only have been borne out of personal conviction. Isaac knew his God. His focus was upon the character of God not upon other people or established institutions. Adult MKs who still struggle with the God-factor of childhood need the help of people who care to similarly focus upon the character of God.

Acknowledging the pain of the MK experience does not negate the richness and joy of the experience any more than it negates a love of God or of one's parents. Adult MKs benefit from sensitive people who will allow any pain to be expressed without judgment. They also benefit from those who will gently guide them to acknowledge that some pain can be exaggerated. Some of the hurdles of childhood are experienced universally or would have been experienced even if the missionary family had not moved abroad. Kind and honest appraisal is a constructive support to the adult MK. In some cases, adult MKs need to be supported as they work through grief or through the process of forgiveness of people they perceive to have hurt them during their childhood years. Those closest to them play a significant role in these areas.

Prayer is a powerful God given resource for intervention into the life of the MK, child or adult. Most missionary parents and concerned adults pray for MKs throughout childhood and during their adult years. The power of the Holy Spirit to protect and guide the MK, child or adult, is unleashed through the intervening prayers of those who care for him or her. The significance and power of this particular intervention cannot be overstated. The privilege of intervention through prayer is a gift from God.

> The privilege of intervention
> through prayer is a gift from God.

When an adult MK evidences a comprehensive understanding and love of God it is a testimony to those around him or her. The legacy of personal conviction can then be passed on to others. If an adult MK will regularly and honestly evaluate his or her own notions of what it is to be a Christian and explore the capacity to hear the prompting of the Holy Spirit, this healthy resolution of the God-factor can become a heritage to be passed on to others.

The MK life holds the potential to draw many people into a comprehensive understanding of God. It holds the potential to model godliness that grows out of personal conviction that God can be trusted to protect and provide even when there is a high cost to a given calling.

God and His Great Commission is the reason for the MK life. The God-factor can be embraced as a powerful by-product of the MK developmental ecology.

Until the return of Christ, the evangelical church will continue to send missionaries abroad in response to the Great Commission. Until Christ returns we will continue to have both child and adult MKs who need to be nurtured, discipled, and cared for. By committing to comprehensively understanding the factors that influence their development, factors that then lead to adult distinctive outcomes, a concerned person can provide constructive intervention and genuine friendship to these individuals. God is pleased when we support one another in the journey through this life.

God is pleased when we support
one another in the journey
through this life.

Appendix

An overview of the Missionary Kids-Consultation and Research Team/Committee on Research and Endowment (MK-CART/CORE)

North American religious mission groups formed a cooperative effort to research the issues of missionary children with the establishment of the Missionary Kids-Consultation and Research Team/Committee on Research and Endowment (MK-CART/CORE). An international conference on missionary kids was held in Manila in 1984 and provided the impetus for organized and cooperative research efforts. A subsequent conference was held in Quito in 1987. The compendia published following the conferences are now out of print. A further conference was held in Nairobi in 1989 where resolutions regarding research were adopted. No compendium was published following the Nairobi conference but some articles are presented in an edited book (Bowers, 1998). The various publications included material from both North Americans and non-North Americans but evidenced the dearth of research on this topic. In 1986 a meeting was held between representatives of eight mission groups and some qualified researchers for the purpose of defining topics requiring research. Thus, MK-CART/CORE was inaugurated. CART was composed of mission representatives who posed questions and identified issues and CORE was made up of 6 researchers responsible for designing and conducting research. The three primary areas identified for the focus of initial research were (a) boarding school personnel and their effect on MK development, (b) the processes and outcomes of MK life, and (c) implications of missionary family life on the development of the MK.

The efforts of the MK CART/CORE have led to a number of publications describing their methodology and findings. The desired outcome of the research has been to understand the dynamics of family life that result in families remaining in the mission work and experiencing healthy relationships inside and outside the family. The desired outcome specific to the MK as dependent minor is to nurture healthy, satisfied children who are spiritually integrated and go on to become mature Christian adults (Powell, 1999).

With these goals established those involved in the multi-mission effort were able to initiate research design. Since its 1986 inception MK CART/CORE has experienced some turnover in participating mission groups and by 1999 a total of 11 mission groups were involved. Three major studies had been conducted: The boarding school personnel study, The adult missionary kid (AMK) study, and The missionary family study. Dr Leslie Andrews, Vice Provost, Director of the Doctor of Ministry Program, and Director of Institutional Research at Asbury Theological Seminary, has been the chair of the research committee since its initial formation.

The boarding school personnel study commenced with a project based on a sampling of those most closely associated with the boarding school situation (Powell & Andrews, 1993). The primary aim of this study was to identify characteristics of effective personnel who could provide a secure environment for the children of missionaries. MK CART/CORE member agencies of the time submitted names of people closely involved in the situation. A sample was compiled including 60 adult MKs, 60 parents of MKs who were then attending or had attended boarding school, and 60 current or previous staff of boarding schools as teachers, house-parents, or administrators. A five-point questionnaire was sent to each member of the sample group. Within each group of 60, 20 individuals were asked to provide responses relating to administrators, 20 relating to teachers, and 20 in relation to boarding house-parents. Four questions were posed asking about qualities, skills, personality traits, and required preparation for effective boarding school personnel. The final point on the questionnaire asked the respondent to describe one person whom they believed to be an effective individual acting in the capacity to which their particular questionnaire related.

A total of 67 surveys was returned (37%), including 27 relating to teachers, 23 to administrators, and 17 to house-parents. From the data researchers identified major themes relating to each category. In the combined data it was established that boarding school personnel, in whatever capacity they work, are more effective if they: (1) possess basic professional skills and knowledge relevant to their work context, (2) exhibit practical Christian understanding and continued advancement in that understanding, (3) have an ability to integrate Christian faith, personal values, and spiritual ideals, (4) evidence a willingness to personally contribute to a community ethos of balance, reasonableness, without a propensity to extremes, and (5) profess a spiritual call to their profession/vocation and to the work context.

A larger study followed and measured a number of variables amongst the entire staff of 20 boarding schools worldwide. Researchers commenced with a list of 129 overseas MK boarding schools representing a total population of 15,000 MKs. Schools were selected to reflect differences in size, sponsorship, and location globally. Researchers traveled to each of the schools to collect data. The data included a demographic questionnaire, subjective practical situation questionnaire, and four standardized instruments. All aimed at gathering information about the characteristics of effective caregivers of children in these circumstances. These were the Minnesota Multiphasic Personality Factor Inventory (MMPI), the Sixteen Personality Factor Test (16PF), the Adjective Check List (ACL), and the Test of Attentional and Interpersonal Style (TAIS). Tests were administered in one five-hour period or during two periods of two and one half hours each. Selected results have been published by various researchers (Taylor & Pollock, 1995; Wickstrom, 1994; Wickstrom & Andrews, 1993).

The major outcome of this research effort has been the inauguration of pre-departure screening and training for boarding school personnel. The Association of Christian

Schools, Interaction Incorporated, and Missionary Internship are three of the organizations who have co-operated to provide this service.

The adult missionary kid study was the largest multi-mission study undertaken. It surveyed adults between the ages of 20 and 80 years. A representative sample was selected from an initial pool of more than 10,000 adult (AMKs). A 40-page questionnaire, including standardized instruments and researcher designed items, was sent to 1,475 individuals. Participants had spent at least three years in a cross-cultural setting because of their parents' role as missionaries. Of the number posted, 259 were returned, undeliverable. A further 25 were returned too late for inclusion in the analysis by Andrews, 1995. This analysis was a measurement of AMKs' well-being. According to Andrews this could best be evaluated by measuring the quality of the AMK's spiritual life. The instrument chosen for this measurement was the Spiritual Well-Being Scale. It was used to measure three dimensions of well-being: religious, existential, and spiritual well-being (Andrews, 1995).

The data from this scale were correlated with variables such as personal characteristics, family culture, education culture, and mission culture domains. Statistical information is provided for 608 participants, 59% of whom are men and 41% are women. Of these 608 participants, 29% have sought professional counseling and a further 20% feel they would benefit from counseling. Associated with family culture, 55% felt included in their parents' ministry. According to Andrews, education is valued by these AMKs because 94% attended college. Of these 73% graduated with a B average or higher and 25% graduated with honors. A total of 11% were listed in the Who's Who in American Colleges and Universities. In terms of mission culture, 17.4% have followed in their parents' paths to become career missionaries. Andrews assesses the overall picture of the AMK in positive terms.

Van Reken (1995) responded to Andrews' analysis of the AMK's spiritual well-being, concerned about the 49% who either had seen or felt they would benefit by seeing a counselor.

In her analysis this represents almost three times as many as the percentage of those who view their missions' community negatively. Therefore, even those who view it positively feel they could benefit from professional assistance in resolving issues from their childhood. Van Reken suggests that the God-factor in the MK's life is a significant variable that needs to be acknowledged. This variable sets the MK apart from other Third Culture Kids. Whereas Andrews assesses adult MK well-being in positive terms Van Reken is more conditional in her appraisal of the data. The mission research team did identify familial connectedness and stability as critical elements in managing the God-factor and nurturing positive MK development. They determined that an understanding of the MK in the family context was important as the next stage in the research efforts.

The missionary family study was designed because of implications arising from the previous two studies. The objective of this research was to study current missionary families, including children in their adolescence and late primary years, in order to develop a profile to better understand missionary families. Research designers intended to obtain demographics as well as descriptions of major activities, family relationships and dynamics, host and mission cultures, areas of satisfaction, and various correlations amongst these variables. Findings were deemed important for training, member/employee care, interventions, and long-term development in mission work. Data collection was via a number of standardized inventories along with researcher designed items and instruments. Data collection and statistical summaries were completed and disseminated to constituent missions in April 1998.

According to the first published findings (Andrews, 1999) participants included 245 missionaries (U.S. in origin), 127 MK adolescents, and 140 MK children. Adult participants were administered the Missionary Family Profile survey including researcher designed measurements of satisfaction, family of origin image, spiritual life inventory, and the standardized family inventory measurements (Olsen, McCubbin, Barnes, Larsen, Muxen & Wilson, 1992).

A researcher designed instrument was administered to the MKs in this study. Included were 14 items measuring parent-adolescent communication, family satisfaction, and family strengths. Findings reportedly indicated MK satisfaction, father closeness, mother closeness, family life satisfaction, and school experience. According to Andrews, MKs expressed positive feelings about MK family life, 89.6% describing it as warm and close or somewhat close. When asked whether they would still choose to be born an MK given what they now know about MK life, 97% responded affirmatively.

The content and stated future direction of the MK CART/CORE projects confirms that the ongoing familial care of members/employees in religious mission work is the motivation for the research. The purpose is to understand the context of MK development within systems (familial, educational, and employment networks) and thereby provide better care and nurture for missionary kids.

Sources:

Andrews, L. A. (1995). Measurement of adult MKs wellbeing. Evangelical Missions Quarterly, 31, 442-446.

Andrews, L. A. (1999). Spiritual family, and ministry satisfaction among missionaries. Journal of Psychology and Theology, 27, 107-118.

Bowers, J. M. (Ed.). (1998). Raising Resilient MKs: Resources for caregivers, parents, and teachers. Colorado Springs, CO: Association of Christian Schools International.

Olsen, D., McCubbin, H. I., Barnes, H., Larsen, A., Muxen, M., & Wilson, M. (1992). Family inventories (2nd rev.). St. Paul, MN: Family Social Science, University of Minnesota.

Powell, J. R. (1999). Families in missions: A research context. Journal of Psychology and Theology, 27, 98-106.

Powell, J. R. & Andrews, L. A. (1993). Qualities desired in MK boarding school personnel: A preliminary study. Journal of Psychology and Theology, 21, 86-92.

Taylor, G. C., & Pollock, D. (1995). Boarding school staff: How to get the best. Evangelical Missions Quarterly, 31, 29-36.

Van Reken, R. E. (1995). Healing the wounded among adult MKs. Evangelical Missions Quarterly, 31, 446-449.

Wickstrom, D. L. (1994). The right stuff in boarding school staff. Evangelical Missions Quarterly, 30, 413-423.

Wickstrom, D. L., & Andrews, L. A. (1993). Personality characteristics of staff members at selected overseas missionary boarding schools. Journal of Psychology and Theology, 18, 332-336.

Notes

Chapter 1

[1] Published material and research findings upon which this work is based:

Cameron, R. (2000, May). "Ecology of child development: The Third Culture kid (TCK) phenomenon." Unpublished manuscript, Griffith University at Mt Gravatt, Queensland.

Cameron, R. (2000, November). Survey responses to TCK pilot survey. Unpublished raw data.

Cameron, R. J. (2003). "The ecology of 'Third Culture Kids': The experiences of Australasian adults." Unpublished doctoral thesis, Murdoch University, Western Australia.

Cottrell, A. B. (1998). "The international education of TCKs." Paper presented to the 1998 Phi Beta Annual Conference, Cholula, Mexico.

Cottrell, A. B. (1999). "Personal manifestations of childhood border crossings: Identity and personality traits of adult TCKs." Paper presented at the Phi Beta Delta 1999 Annual Conference, San Diego, California.

Cottrell, A. B. (2002). "Educational & occupational choices of American ATCKs", in M. G. Ender. (Ed.). *Military Brats and other Global Nomads: Growing up in organization families,* 229-253. Westport, Connecticut: Praeger.

Pollock, D. C., & Van Reken, R. E. (1999). *Third Culture Kids: The experience of growing up among worlds.* London: Nicholas Brealey Publishing.

Useem, R. H., & Cottrell, A. B. (January 1993). "Third Culture kids: Focus of major study", in *NewsLinks: The newspaper of International Schools Services,* XII (3).

Useem, R. H., & Cottrell, A. B. (1993, May). "TCKs four times more likely to earn bachelor's degree", in *NewsLinks: The newspaper of International Schools Services*, XII (5).

Useem, R. H., & Cottrell, A. B. (1993, November). "ATCKs have problems relating to own ethnic groups", in *NewsLinks: The newspaper of International Schools Services*, XIII (2).

Useem, R. H., & Cottrell, A. B. (1994, March). "ATCKs maintain global dimensions throughout their lives", in *NewsLinks: The newspaper of International Schools Services*, XIII (4).

These works by no means represent a comprehensive bibliography of the material that is available to substantiate the existence of the Third Culture Kid (TCK) phenomenon or the Missionary Kid (MK) subcategory of this phenomenon. These works are listed here as the primary sources that have been used to triangulate the credibility of the author's, research findings. The findings of these other significant writers and researchers, Useem and Cottrell, Pollock and Van Reken, have been cross-referenced with the findings of Cameron, and only those findings that have been so confirmed have been included for commentary in this book. The works of each of these authors has incorporated the broader TCK phenomenon and reference has been made to MKs as a significant subcategory.

A notable amount of research and writing has been undertaken specifically related to issues impacting MKs through a cooperative mission agency effort. A summary of the efforts and resulting works of the Missionary Kids-Consultation and Research Team/Committee on Research and Endowment (MK-CART/CORE) is included as an Appendix.

Chapter 2

[1] Third Culture Kid (TCK) definition:

Useem, R. H., & Cottrell, A. B. (1993, January). "Third Culture kids: Focus of major study", in *NewsLinks: The newspaper of International Schools Services*, XII (3).

It was in the 1950s that Dr Ruth Useem and her husband first observed the uniqueness of children growing up abroad, while they were undertaking anthropological work in India. The term Third Culture Kids (TCKs) was coined. Anthropologists and sociologists began to purposefully study the phenomenon and in recent times others with a vested interest in the outcomes of a childhood spent abroad have been drawn to the study.

[2] Definition of culture as a learned way of living:

Schultz, E. A. & Lavenda, R. H. (1998). *Cultural anthropology: A perspective on the human condition* (4th ed.). Mountain View, California: Mayfield Publishing Company.

Schultz and Lavenda describe culture as learned behavior that human beings acquire as they function as members within a given group or context. Culture then, does not have location related parameters nor is it bound to a given people group. With this definition, culture is a set of behavioral patterns that can be acquired by any person who is within a given context, or amongst a given people group. The behaviors are learned as a response to the demands of life. This preferred definition allows the culture of Third Culture Kids to be a culture because it is an accumulation of behaviors learned in response to their life patterns. These patterns are experienced no matter what is their passport country or host country.

[3] Early definitions of the Third Culture as an intersection of cultures:

Jordan, K. A. F. (1981). "The adaptation process of Third Culture dependent youth as they re-enter The United States and enter college: An exploratory study." Unpublished doctoral thesis, Michigan State University.

Salmon, J. L. (1987). "The relationship of stress and mobility to the psychosocial development and well-being of third-culture-reared early adults." Unpublished doctoral thesis, The Florida State University.

The earliest researchers of the Third Culture Kid phenomenon presumed that the unique outcomes of the TCK experience resulted from a partial assimilation into the cultures of each of the countries within which they were immersed. Usually this was the passport country culture and the host country culture. The early assumption was that the TCK absorbed a part of each culture and therefore represented an overlap between the two cultures.

[4] Definition of culture as styles of life (within **Figure 2.1**):

Schultz, E. A. & Lavenda, R. H. (1998). *Cultural anthropology: A perspective on the human condition* (4th ed.). Mountain View, California: Mayfield Publishing Company.

Culture, which is learned behavior, (see Note number 2, Chapter 2), leads to styles of life created and shared by members of a given society. When members of a given society learn similar behavior patterns it shapes their styles of life and creates group cohesion. This cohesion facilitates the affinity that is shared between Third Culture Kids, and indeed Missionary Kids, no matter where their childhood years have been spent or what is their passport country.

[5] **Figure 2.2** An adapted model, proposed to depict the Third Culture Kid (TCK) ecology of human development.

Cameron, R. J. (2003). "The ecology of 'Third Culture Kids': The experiences of Australasian adults." Unpublished doctoral thesis, Murdoch University, Western Australia.

This model was first presented in the doctoral dissertation of the author, Cameron. The language has been modified slightly for presentation in this book so that it more explicitly reflects the Missionary Kid (MK) ecology of development rather than the general Third Culture Kid (TCK) ecology of development.

Chapter 3

[1] **Table 3.1** Defining elements of the MK ecology and the associated potentially positive and potentially negative outcomes.

The list of references included for Note number 1, Chapter 1, represent those that were used to compile this table. The table documents the most significant elements of the Missionary Kid (MK) developmental ecology and the related eventual outcomes in the adult profile of the individual.

Chapter 5

[1] The God-factor:

Van Reken, R. E. (1995). "Healing the wounded among adult MKs", in *Evangelical Missions Quarterly 31*, 446-449.

Ruth Van Reken first coined the term the God-factor on behalf of adult Missionary Kids to allow them to acknowledge that God is at the center of the Missionary Kid (MK) life. The term effectively encompasses the concept that God is the reason for the MK life. The term embodies the understanding that MKs have the chance to develop an early and comprehensive spiritual awareness; it embodies an understanding that the pain of sacrifice demanded by the missionary family life is legitimate. While it allows that the pain is legitimate it also allows that it is possible to reconcile this pain without denying God. The very acknowledgement that there is a God-factor releases an individual to explore a relationship with a loving God that matures and grows out of personal conviction.

Chapter 6

[1] Inherited predispositions:

Bouchard, T. J. Jr. (1998). "Genetic and environmental influences on intelligence and special mental abilities", in *Human Biology 70*, 257-279.

Bouchard, T. J. Jr, Lykken, D. T., McGue, M., Segal, N. L. & Tellegen, A. (1990). "Sources of human psychological differences: The Minnesota study of twins reared apart", in *Science*, 250, 223(6).

Piaget, J. (1970). "Piaget's theory", in P. Mussen (Ed.), *Handbook of child psychology* (3rd ed.). New York: Wiley.

Plomin, R., & McClearn, G. E. (Eds.). (1993). *Nature, nurture and psychology*. Washington D.C: American Psychological Association.

Steen, R. G. (1996). *DNA and destiny: Nature and nurture in human behavior*. New York: Plenum Press.

Vygotsky, L.S. (1978). *Mind in society: The development of higher mental process*. Cambridge, Massachusetts: Harvard University Press.

Vygotsky, L.S. (1986). *Thought and language*. Cambridge, Massachusetts: MIT Press.

Vygotsky, L.S. (1997). *Educational psychology*. Boca Raton, Florida: St. Lucie Press.

Nature and nurture each have significant effects on child development. The Swiss psychologist, Jean Piaget proposed developmental stages that children progress through according to nature's course. He identified four factors that interact to influence development, or progression to a successive cognitive stage – biological maturation, activity, social experience, and equilibration (the search for balance between cognitive schemes and information in the environment) (Piaget, 1970). The influence of nature and nurture are apparent in the theories proposed by Piaget. Lev Vygotsky was a Russian theorist whose propositions support those of Piaget, however, he suggested that development is much more strongly influenced by the people in a developing child's world. He suggested that knowledge, ideas, attitudes, and values develop through interaction with others. Vygotsky made special comment on the role and importance of language during interaction, to the nurture process (Vygotsky, 1978, 1986, 1997). Therefore the social environment in which a child is nurtured plays a key role in development.

Ongoing studies are being carried out through the University of Minnesota's Center for Twin and Adoption Research. Through this center research is being conducted on identical twins who have been split at birth and raised in different environments to suggest aspects of development that are affected by inheritance and by environment (Bouchard, 1998; McGue & Bouchard, 1998). One of the main difficulties with conducting research in this field is the relatively small population of identical twins reared separately and available for study. However, in recent years, researchers have combined their data to give findings more credibility (Steen, 1996). Moreover, twins who have been separated but have continued to share some parts of the same environment have been sifted out of the combined data. Current findings, therefore, are adequate to establish that inherited traits and the environment interact in the emergence of a person's character (Bouchard, Lykken, McGue, Segal & Tellegen, 1990). Personality traits of identical twins have been distributed fairly evenly in the interaction of nature (heritability) and nurture (environment).

This work accepts the researched findings that support a genetic basis of variation in development, and goes on to concentrate on the possible consequences of one source of variation in the environment – that of major changes in the physical and social culture within which the child is being raised.

[2] Dyadic relationships:

Bronfenbrenner, U. (1979). *The ecology of human development: Experiments by nature and design*. Cambridge: Harvard University Press.

Primary dyads are relationships between two people where members continue in each other's thoughts and continue to influence each other's behavior and choices even when they are not together. Dyadic relationships in the immediate setting exert greatest influence on the child.

[3] Missionary Kid (MK) dyadic relationship data:

Cameron, R. J. (2003). "The ecology of "Third Culture Kids": The experiences of Australasian adults." Unpublished doctoral thesis, Murdoch University, Western Australia, 273.

Raw data collected by the author, Cameron, provided evidence of the dyadic relationships considered significant by the adult Missionary Kids involved in this study. The data were separated to reflect those who had experienced a boarding school environment during childhood and those who had remained with their immediate family during the missionary experience. The data also reflect the dyads that were deemed significant within the immediate context and those that were significant in a broader social network for these MKs.

Frequency of reference to influential dyadic relationships and social networks within the TCK ecology, by subcategories: boarder and non-boarders

TOTAL DATA [n = 45]							
BOARDERS (n = 14)				NON-BOARDERS (n = 31)			
DYADIC RELATIONSHIPS		WIDER SOCIAL NETWORKS		DYADIC RELATIONSHIPS		WIDER SOCIAL NETWORKS	
Dorm parents	10	Parents	8	Parents	29	Grandparents	13
Siblings	2	Siblings	3	Siblings	17	Cousins	2
Domestic workers	3	Parents' host country national working peers	4	Domestic workers	16	Relatives in passport country	10
Teachers	11	Grandparents	4	Host country neighborhood children	14	Social contacts at expatriate recreational club	7
Peers in dorms	9	Relatives in passport country	3	Teachers	23	Siblings living elsewhere	2
Classmates	5	Host country national children	3	Parents' host country national working peers	9	Sponsor agency directors	1
		Sponsor agency directors	1	Expatriate friends	19	Older siblings of expatriate friends (when home)	1
		Tourists	1	Expatriate adult friends within sponsor agency	9		
		Expatriate adult friends within sponsor agency	3	Other expatriate adults	8		
		Other expatriate adults	2				

Chapter 7

[1] Social development theory:

Laible, D., Carlo, G., & Raffaelli, M. (2000). "The differential impact of parent and peer attachment on adolescent adjustment", in *Journal of Youth and Adolescence, 29*, 45-59.

Van Lieshout, C. F. M., & Doise, W. (1998). "Social development", in A. De metriou, W. Doise, and C. Van Lieshout. (Eds.) *Life-span developmental psychology* (271-316). Chichester: John Wiley and Sons.

Social development occurs within the context of a child's home and wider environment. It is a gradual process during which there is an emerging autonomy and yet a retained connection with parents and significant other persons in a child's life (Laible, Carlo, & Raffaelli, 2000). Peer attachment also plays a significant role in social development and this may be in different domains to the areas of parental influence, according to these authors. It is important to recognize the different roles played so as to understand interactions between a person and a context. This is the case in any ecology but more so where ecologies are to be compared according to their impact on child development.

Groups are said to play a significant role in social development. Groups provide systems of shared meaning, group goals, behavioral regulation, and emotional exchange beyond that of interpersonal relationships. Both family groups, and peer groups within schools play a significant role in a child's social development (Van Lieshout & Doise, 1998).

[2] Hierarchy of social groups and the impact on emerging social autonomy:

Degirmencioglu, S. M., Urberg, K. A., Tolson, J. M., & Rao, P. (1998). "Adolescent friendship networks: Continuity and change over the school year", in *Merrill Palmer Quarterly, 44*, 313-337.

Laible, D., Carlo, G., & Raffaelli, M. (2000). "The differential impact of parent and peer attachment on adolescent adjustment", in *Journal of Youth and Adolescence, 29*, 45-59.

As a child develops there is an emerging autonomy from the family. However, Liable, Carlo, and Raffaelli (2000), claim that the most positive adjustment occurs when there is a secure relationship with both parents, and peers. During person-context interactions parents gradually exert less influence over an adolescent child and peers begin to influence development and adjustment in areas such as management of aggression, sympathy, and depression. These influences are enduring if there is continuity in proximal contexts (Degirmencioglu, Urberg, Tolson, and Richard, 1998). According to these authors if there is an early and persistent exposure to behavior patterns this may be critical to continuity of those patterns throughout the life course. Continuity in networks and the resultant continuity in demands from close friends can have the effect of reinforcing behavior patterns and reinforcing identity. There are multiple levels in social networks and therefore, multiple levels of influence. According to Degirmencioglu et al., most adolescents have one best friend, a number of close friends, and a friendship group that may or may not include all of those close friends. They represent a hierarchy of influence exerted over the child in the peer network.

However, they acknowledge that little is known about the effect on individual members when a group dissolves. In the Missionary Kid (MK) context this is experienced early in a child's life and repeatedly experienced as expatriate families move in and out of MK ecologies. A friendship group may not dissolve entirely but the dynamics of social interaction are altered as members leave and others are initiated. In the networks studied by Degirmencioglu et al. childhood friendships changed gradually. Where a child may have had a dyadic relationship with one friend before a school break, there may have been some shift in relational patterns after the break but the dyad moved gradually to a networked social friendship in the next strata of the social hierarchy. For the MK this can be the experience but many times the relational patterns and social network changes are abrupt changes. New children arrive in an expatriate community throughout the school year, dependent on when their parents commence a new contract. Children leave just as abruptly at the termination of parental contracts. Children within the MK social network live with the awareness of the temporal nature of their residence in any expatriate community and it can be seen to impact on their social behaviors.

Other factors that may impact a gradual increase in autonomy within person-context for the MK are the differing roles played across diverse social groups, and for MKs in boarding school, the intermittent interaction with immediate family members. MKs move between settings where the social make up is primarily passport country expatriates, to settings where the social make up is multi-cultural, and to other settings where the MK may be the only non-national present. Demands on social behavior may change rapidly.

The boarding school experience requires the MK to move regularly, throughout the year, between being fairly autonomous and personally responsible, to being part of the nuclear family. An MK may experience boarding home equality of demands and responsibilities as one child amongst many during the term and then go home to the behaviors and conduct expected of a birth order ranking. Parents may maintain past expectations on the child, unaware of gradual shifts in relational patterns that occur during a ten-week term or an eleven-month year, depending on how long the child is absent. Within these dyadic relationships the shift in power and altered behaviors can occur in irregular jumps rather than gradual shifts. The gradual shift in social patterns, and the gradual increase in demands from family members and close friendships that can reinforce behavior patterns may not be the experience of the MK. However, the patterns that do occur may be seen to influence social development through an alternative trajectory.

[3] Time – cumulative and point of impact as significant to childhood:

Elder, G. H. Jr. (1998). "The life course as developmental theory", in *Child Development, 69(1)*, 1-12.

The principle of timing in lives refers to the developmental impact of a succession of life transitions or events in a person's life within the available options. Elder (1998), presents a model for describing human development that suggests four principles of development: historical time and place (establishing context of development), timing in lives (cumulative impact of events occurring early and late), linked lives (dyadic connections), and human agency (individual's successful adaptation and active choices).

Individuals construct their own life course through the choices and actions they take within the opportunities afforded by historical time and social circumstances. The events of life and choices made happen at significant times and mark the life trajectory of the child. Sometimes the timing of an event or a choice is of greater significance than at other times. However, events and choices happen in succession throughout childhood and gradually build up to have an accumulated impact on development.

In the case of the Missionary Kid (MK) parental career choice has a significant impact on the available options in the MK environment. Choices and events occur within these boundaries. The move overseas dictates the social circumstances of development. Furthermore, mandates of the deploying agency can impinge on opportunities. Educational opportunities are restricted to what is available, is of an acceptable standard, and is within the funding limits of the sponsor agency. MKs can be restricted by moral and social codes regulating conduct. In some circumstances personal choice, or exercising human agency, potentially affect ongoing parental employment or promotional opportunities. Timing, both point of impact and cumulative, is a significant factor in the MK developmental ecology.

Chapter 8

[1] Self-awareness leading to self-management:

Goleman, D., Boyatzis, R. & McKee, A. (2002). *Primal Leadership: Realizing the power of emotional intelligence*. Boston, MA: Harvard Business School Press.

Authors who write on the topic of emotional intelligence refer to the concepts of self-awareness and self-management. Goleman, Boyatzis, and McKee (2002) describe self-awareness as the capacity to understand one's emotions and be clear about one's purpose. From this understanding and clarity, flows self-management. An individual who knows what he or she is feeling will then be able to manage those feelings. The individual has the capacity to manage emotions rather than having emotion control him or her. By staying in control of one's feelings and impulses, an individual has the capacity to shape an environment of trust, comfort, and fairness.

[2] Personality profiling resources:

Professional Dynametric Programs. (1978). Woodland Park CO., PDP, INC.

Professional Dynametric Programs® or PDP is a personality profiling resource that has been validated for use with individuals from the age of twelve years. It has been successfully used with children and teens as well as with adults to help them to understand their own personalities, energy levels, preferred communication styles, and interaction patterns. It is one possible resource that can be used as part of constructive intervention to help Missionary Kids (MKs) increase in self-awareness and therefore to establish behaviors that enhance self-management.

[3] Gradual shifts in power within chosen relationships between child and adult:

Barone, C., Iscoe, E., Trickett, E. J. & Schmid, K. D. (1998). "An ecologically differentiated, multifactor model of adolescent network orientation", in *American Journal of Community Psychology, 26 (3),* 403-423.

Franco, N. & Levitt, M. J. (1998). "The social ecology of middle childhood: Family support, friendship quality, and self-esteem", in *Family Relations, 47(4),* 315-321.

Some authors have described the importance of non-family members in the socialization process (Barone, Iscoe, Trickett & Schmid, 1998; Franco and Levitt, 1998). Barone et al. describe family and friends as the first two significant social networks in a child's ecology, and adults outside the nuclear family unit as representing the third network. These adults may be found in work settings and can help the socialization process by offering advice or acting as role models. Franco and Levitt suggest that it can be non-parental adults who fill this role in the socialization process. These and other friendships can be significant in building self-definition and self-worth because they are chosen relationships and not obligated ones as with familial relationships. For the Missionary Kid (MK) these relationships may be found within the sponsor agency community or the wider expatriate community. However, the temporal nature of these relationships is, once again, an inhibiting factor in learning gradual shifts in power and increasing levels of trust built over time. The maturing process resulting in broad social competence can be challenged.

Chapter 9

[1] Identity securing talismans:

Iyer, P. (2000). *The global soul: Jet lag, shopping malls, and the search for home.* New York: Alfred. A. Knopf.

One author, focusing on internationally oriented life patterns, refers to himself as a Global Soul who has no fixed community to call home but rather carries precious identity-securing talismans about with him and has a kinship with others who share a common lifestyle (Iyer, 2000). The Missionary Kid (MK) may accumulate representative objects that reflect the complexity of his or her life.